Creating Graphics for Avid Xpress DV 3.5
with Adobe Photoshop 7

Copyright and Disclaimer

Contents

Module 2: Importing and Exporting Still Graphics

Exercise 2: Importing Still Graphics

Module 3: Creating Alpha Channels

Exercise 3: Creating Alpha Channels

Module 4: Editing with Alpha Channels

Exercise 4: Using Alpha Channels in Effects

Module 5: Using Photoshop Layers

Exercise 5: Working with Layers

Module 6: Creating Layer Styles and Actions

Exercise 6: Working with Layer Styles

Module 7: Preparing EPS and PDF Files for Import

Exercise 7: Converting EPS and PDF Files

Module 8: Importing and Exporting Video

Appendix A: Preparing Video for the Internet

Index

Preface

About This Course

This course was developed by the award-winning team of Avid course developers and education specialists to provide you with an in-depth overview of the concepts and techniques necessary to create a effects on an Avid Xpress DV. It documents step-by-step procedures for all basic effect operations, providing many screen captures and explanatory notes as aids to learning.

Instructions for copying the files from the CD-ROM to your computer are found at the end of the Preface and in a Read Me file on the CD itself. If you experience any difficulty installing the CD-ROM or loading the files from it, contact Avid Educational Services at edservices@avid.com.

Who Should Take This Course

This course provides sufficiently detailed instructions on how to create graphics for use with the Avid Xpress DV system and is designed for the beginner to intermediate user.

You should have basic familiarity with the editing and effects capabilities of the system. Participants may be online editors, freelance editors, staff editors, film editors, or online effect designers.

Course Prerequisites

This course assumes that you have a basic understanding of Xpress DV and have taken the Avid Xpress DV 3 Editing and the Introduction to Avid Xpress DV 3 Effects courses. It also assumes that you are familiar with the Windows or Macintosh computer system software, whichever one you use.

Course Structure and Special Features

This course alternates between informational modules and self-paced exercises. In the modules, a combination of conceptual material, step-by-step procedures, and illustrations is used to teach the creation of effects with the Xpress DV system. Tips and warnings provide useful guidance along the way. Review questions are found at the end of each module. If you are unsure of the correct answer to any question, you should review the appropriate material in the course before continuing to the exercise or the next module.

At the back of the book you will find an index to help you locate specific items, and a list of courseware developed by Avid Technology.

Avid Educational Series

The Avid Educational Series consists of an extensive range of instructor-led courses and self-study materials developed by Avid Educational Services. You will find a complete list at the back of the book.

You might find the course listed below particularly appropriate for your next learning opportunity.

- Color Correction for Avid Xpress DV

  This course is available both as an instructor-led course or as a stand-alone book with exercise media on CD-ROM.

For More Information

For information about Avid courseware, schedules of up-coming classes, locations of Avid Authorized Education Centers, how to order self-paced books and CDs, visit the Avid website, www.avid.com/training. In addition, to find out more about Avid Educational Services offerings from within North America, call 800 867 AVID (2843), or from elsewhere, call 978 275-2071.

To purchase Avid Educational Services books or CDs from the Avid Store, visit www.avidstore.com.

If you would like to see additional documentation on the use of your system, refer to (or order) the User's Guide for your system. To place an order from within the United States, call Avid Telesales at 800-949-AVID, or from outside the United States, contact your local Avid sales representative.

This Book's Symbols and Conventions

This guide uses the following special symbols and conventions:

1. Numbered lists, when *order* is important.

    b. Alphabetical lists (within numbered lists), when *order* is important.

    • Bulleted lists, when the order of the items is unimportant.

■ Single step directions when only one step is required.

IMPORTANT comments are written in boldface.

▲ **WARNING is a special type of Important comment. It is set off by this symbol and describes a warning associated with the feature, possibly to avoid.**

✍ *TIP describes a tip, related step, or an alternative way to perform an action. It is set off by this symbol and is in italics.*

Avid Systems and Computer Platforms

This course book applies to both Windows® XP and Macintosh® systems. Most Avid interface windows and tools look the same on both systems, most procedures are identical, and most menu items and keystrokes are the same. For significant differences, the book includes both the Windows and Macintosh versions. Throughout the course book, references to Windows stand for Windows XP.

The following table provides the most frequently used equivalent keys and buttons for Macintosh and Windows systems:

Table 1: Windows/Macintosh Equivalents

Windows	Macintosh
Control (Ctrl)	Command
Alt	Option
Enter key on the main (not numeric) keypad	Return key
Backspace	Delete
Close button (X in upper-right corner of a window)	Close box in upper-left corner of a window to close a window
Control+click multiple items in a window, or click the first item and Shift+click the last item in a range	Shift+click multiple items in a window
C: drive	Avid drive (internal hard drive)

Copying the Files from Course CD-ROM

The CD-ROM that accompanies this book contains media formatted for the Avid Xpress DV system. It should not be used on any other Avid system.

The files on this CD-ROM are compatible with both the Windows XP and the Macintosh OS X versions of Avid Xpress DV.

 If you are installing this media on a Windows system, there are additional steps required beyond simply copying the media to the system. Please see the instructions later in this section.

This CD contains the following:

- **Avid Projects** — contains the project you will use with this course, Creating Graphics.

- **Graphics** — contains the graphics used in the exercises.

- **OMFI MediaFiles** — contains the media required for the course.

Copying the Files to Your System:

Windows:

On the CD, open the Avid Projects folder. Copy the folder you find inside (Creating Graphics) to the C:/Program Files/Avid/Avid Xpress DV/Avid Projects. (If the Avid folder is on a drive other than the C: drive, copy to that Avid folder.)

To copy the Media Files, you have a couple of options:

- If your drive already has an *OMFI MediaFiles* folder, you can open the CD's *OMFI MediaFiles* folder and copy the contents into your existing folder. OR:

- If your drive does not have an *OMFI MediaFiles* folder, copy the entire *OMFI MediaFiles* folder from the CD to your drive.

Macintosh:

On the CD, open the Avid Projects folder. Copy the folder you find inside (Creating Graphics) to the Avid Projects folder on your internal hard drive. (If the Avid folder is on an external drive, copy to that folder.)

To copy the Media Files, you have a couple of options:

- If your drive already has an *OMFI MediaFiles* folder, you can open the CD's *OMFI MediaFiles* folder and copy the contents into your existing folder. OR:

- If your drive does not have an *OMFI MediaFiles* folder, copy the entire *OMFI MediaFiles* folder from the CD to your drive.

Opening the Project Files

The course book describes how to open and use the projects on this disc. However, if you didn't install Avid Xpress DV in the default location, then the first time you open a project in Avid Xpress DV, you will see the following message:

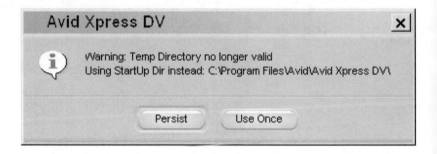

Click Persist, and Avid Xpress DV handles the rest. You will not see this message again.

Note for Windows Users:

If you are using a Windows system, additional steps are required after you have copied the project and media onto the system.

Files and folders stored on a CD-ROM are marked as "Read-Only" by Windows. When the files are copied to a hard drive, the Read-Only status is maintained. Though it is preferred for media files to remain Read-Only to prevent you from accidentally deleting them, the project files and folders *cannot* be Read-Only.

To remove the Read Only status from the project files:

1. Open Windows Explorer.

2. Navigate to: C:/Program Files/Avid/Avid Xpress DV/Avid Projects. (If you copied the projects to another location, navigate to that location instead.)

3. In the Avid Projects folder, select the Creating Graphics project.

4. Right-click on the folder and select Properties from the bottom of the pop-up menu.

5. The Properties dialog box appears.

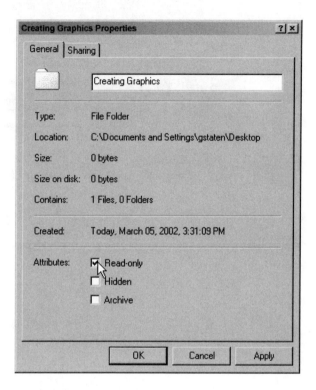

6. Deselect "Read-Only" and click OK.

7. The Confirm Attribute Changes dialog box appears.

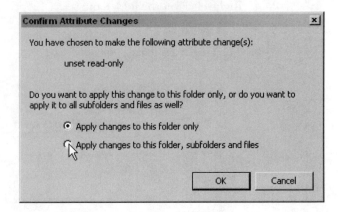

8. Select the option, "Apply changes to this folder, subfolders and files" and click OK.

The projects are now ready for you to use!

Creating Graphics for Avid Xpress DV 3.5

Overview

Designed for the advanced Avid Xpress DV editor, this course demonstrates how to prepare still and moving graphics in Adobe® Photoshop® for import into Avid Xpress DV.

Goals

After you complete of this course, you will be able to:

- Prepare still graphics, including images with alpha channels, in Adobe Photoshop for import into Avid Xpress DV

- Create soft drop shadows, glows, and video bevels for titles and graphics

- Import and export still graphics, video, and sequential files into and out of Avid Xpress DV

Class Outline

Module 1:   **Preparing Still Graphics**

- Preparing to Import
- Preparing Graphics
- Saving the File
- Optional File Modifications

Exercise 1:   *Preparing Still Graphics*

- Preparing the Files

Module 2:   **Importing and Exporting Still Graphics**

- Supported File Types
- Importing Still Graphic Files
- Changing the Duration of an Imported Still
- Exporting Still Frames from Avid Xpress DV

Exercise 2:   *Importing Still Graphics*

- Importing the Files

Module 3:   **Creating Alpha Channels**

- Creating Alpha Channels with Adobe Photoshop
- Using the Magic Wand Tool
- Using Quick Mask Mode
- Touching Up a Previously Saved Alpha Channel

Exercise 3:   *Creating Alpha Channels*

- Creating the Alpha Channels

Module 4:   Editing with Alpha Channels

- Importing Graphics with Alpha Channels
- Modifying an Imported Matte Key's Contents

Exercise 4:   *Using Alpha Channels in Effects*

- Importing Matte Keys
- Creating a Graphic Wipe
- Using an Alpha Channel as a Custom Wipe
- Creating a Graphic Wipe
- Creating a Hold-Out Matte

Module 5:   Using Photoshop Layers

- Working with Layers
- Working with Type Layers
- Working with Multiple Layers
- Saving Files with Layers
- Importing Layered Files into Avid Xpress DV

Exercise 5:   *Working with Layers*

- Creating a Safe Title/Action Grid Overlay
- Experimenting with Text Layers

Module 6:   Creating Layer Styles and Actions

- Creating Beveled Text and Graphics
- Creating a Drop Shadow
- Creating a Glow
- Creating a Video Bevel
- Using Photoshop Actions

Module 1

Preparing Still Graphics

Avid Xpress DV allows you to import many different kinds of files. This module focuses on importing still graphics into Avid Xpress DV.

Objectives

After you complete this module, you will be able to:

- Identify the criteria that your file must meet to import it into Avid Xpress DV

- Prepare images for import into Avid Xpress DV by changing the size, resolution, color mode, and format within Adobe Photoshop

Preparing to Import

For best results, still graphics must meet a specific set of criteria before you import them into Avid Xpress DV. The following section describes these criteria, and the parameters they involve.

Criteria for Import

Frame Size

All graphics and animations should be properly sized for import. If not, it is likely that the image will be distorted and the quality reduced. The following table lists the proper NTSC and PAL frame sizes for imported graphics and animations that will be imported into Avid Xpress DV.

Format	4x3 Aspect Ratio Square Pixel	16x9 Aspect Ratio Square Pixel	Native Size[†] Non-Square Pixel
NTSC	640 x 480	853 x 480	720 x 480
PAL	768 x 576	1024 x 576	720 x 576

[†] *Native size refers to the actual frame size stored internally by the editing system. These sizes conform to the industry specifications for digital video. These sizes are discussed in greater detail in Module 8.*

Color Space

This is how the image data is stored within the file. In Photoshop this is often referred to as *color mode*. Common modes include Bitmap, Grayscale, Index, RGB, and CMYK.

■ Save files as RGB.

Other color modes may not import correctly or generate errors when importing.

Format

Avid Xpress DV accepts a variety of file formats. The most commonly used formats are TIFF, PICT, and Photoshop.

✍ *See "Supported File Types" on page 2-2 for a description of the major supported file formats.*

Preparing Graphics

The first step is to turn on the computer and launch Adobe Photoshop.

Launching Adobe Photoshop

■ Locate the Adobe Photoshop program and double-click it to launch the program.

✍ *To easily launch Adobe Photoshop, or any other application, right-click (Windows) or Control+click (Macintosh) on the program icon and select Create Shortcut (Windows) or Make Alias (Macintosh) from the menu. Then drag the alias to the desktop where you can access it readily.*

Configuring Adobe Photoshop

Photoshop has many options which should be configured properly before creating graphics for video. The default configurations are suitable for graphics creation for the web or for print, but are not appropriate for video graphics.

1. Open the Color Settings by choosing Edit > Color Settings (Windows) or Photoshop > Color Settings (Macintosh).

   The default color configuration is optimized for Web graphics. This configuration can result in color shifts in video graphics, especially those exported from Avid Xpress DV.

2. Select **Color Management Off** from the Settings pop-up menu.

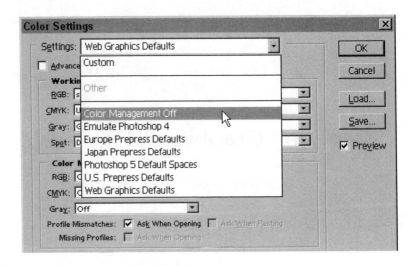

3. Click OK to close the dialog.

4. Open the Units and Rulers settings by choosing Edit > Preferences > Units & Rulers (Windows) or Photoshop > Preferences > Units & Rulers (Macintosh).

5. Select pixels from the Rulers pop-up menu.

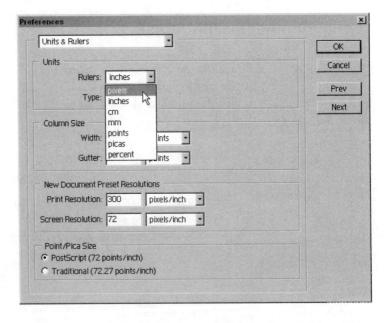

6. Click OK to close the dialog.

Opening a File

1. Choose File > Open.

2. Navigate through the file directory to locate the folder that contains the files you need to prepare.

3. Select a file and click Open.

Zooming In or Out on an Image

Zooming in or out on an image lets you see more or less detail.

To zoom in on an image:

■ Type Control++ (Windows) or Command++ (Macintosh).

Repeat until you reach the desired detail level.

✍ *If you type Control+Alt++ (Windows) or Command+Option++ (Macintosh), the window will be resized along with the image.*

To zoom out on an image:

■ Type Control+− (Windows) or Command+− (Macintosh).

Repeat until you reach the desired detail level.

✍ *If you type Control+Alt+− (Windows) or Command+Option+− (Macintosh), the window will be resized along with the image.*

Moving around a zoomed-in image:

■ Press and hold the Space bar.

The cursor changes to a hand. Drag the hand to move the image within the window to see areas that are out of view.

Determining the Image Size and Color Mode

After you open a file in Adobe Photoshop, the Size Preview box allows you to determine the image dimensions and color mode. Check this box any time you plan to import an image into Avid Xpress DV.

1. (Windows) Point the cursor to the second box from the left at the bottom of Photoshop's main window.

(Macintosh) Point the cursor to the second box from the lower-left corner of the graphic file's window.

2. Hold down the Alt key (Windows) or the Option key (Macintosh) and press the mouse button down.

The width, height, channels, color mode, and resolution of the image appear.

Width: 1459 pixels (6.632 inches)
Height: 989 pixels (4.495 inches)
Channels: 3 (RGB Color)
Resolution: 220 pixels/inch

Cropping the Image to the Proper Size

In most cases, the image is not at the size or aspect ratio required for import. Photoshop provides a Crop tool that makes it easy to resize the image.

Configuring the Crop Tool

You can customize many of the tools in Adobe Photoshop. The Crop tool allows you to specify the target width and height for the image.

1. Select the Crop tool in the Tool Palette.

 You can also press the C key on the keyboard to activate it.

The options for the selected tool are displayed at the top of the screen below the menu bar.

✍ *If the options are missing, display them by choosing Window > Show Options.*

2. Enter the appropriate height and width into the width and height fields.

Format	4x3 Aspect Ratio	16x9 Aspect Ratio
NTSC	640 x 480	853 x 480
PAL	768 x 576	1024 x 576

Cropping the Image

1. Select the crop region by clicking and dragging the Crop tool from one corner of the desired region diagonally across to the opposite corner of the desired region.

   A rectangular box displays around the borders of the selection and the region outside of the selection is dimmed. Notice how the aspect ratio of the crop region is locked to the video aspect ratio you specified by setting the target width and the height in the Crop options.

2. If necessary, adjust the selected region using one of the following methods.

   a. To resize the selection, drag the handle in one of the corners of the selection.

   b. To move the selection, click within the region and drag it to a new location.

c. To rotate the selection, position the cursor just beyond one of the corners of the selection, and click and drag to rotate the selection.

d. To delete the region and start over, press the Escape key and create the selection again.

▲ **Try not to crop the image too close to the edges of the foreground object. Portions of the image that lie beyond the Safe Action area may not appear on a consumer television. The Safe Action area is 10 percent in from the edge of the active picture area.**

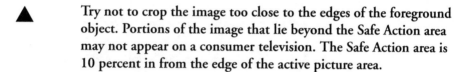

3. Press the Enter key to perform the crop.

The image is cropped to the size you specified in the Crop options.

4. While holding down the Alt key (Windows) or the Option key (Macintosh), press the Size Preview box to verify that the new image parameters are correct.

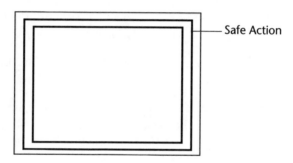

Saving the File

You specify the file format when you save the file. You can save the file in a variety of file formats including TIFF, PICT and Photoshop.

1. Choose File > Save As.

   Use the Save As option instead of the Save option. Doing so will leave the original uncropped file on your system in the event you need to recompose the image at a later date.

2. If necessary, navigate to the folder you wish to save the files in.

   You might want to create a work folder to save your final images.

3. Append the file name to indicate that the file is properly sized for import.

   A good option is to add a dash and the width the image was cropped to, for example -640 or -768.

4. Choose the desired file format from the list of formats in the Format pop-up menu and click Save.

   Depending upon the format chosen, an additional dialog may appear. The following section describes the dialogs for TIFF and PICT files. (No additional dialog appears for Photoshop files.)

- TIFF format:

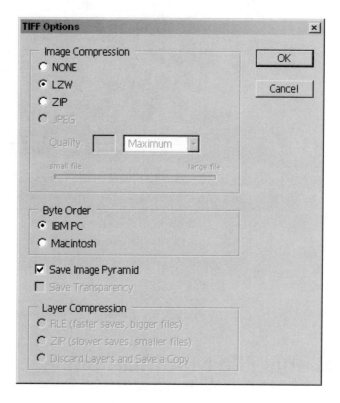

a. Choose LZW Compression.

LZW compression is a lossless compression. With lossless compression, images do not lose detail when compressed, maintaining the integrity of the image.

b. Click OK.

Photoshop saves the new file to the selected destination.

- PICT format:

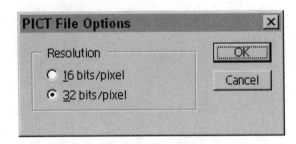

a. Choose 32 bits/pixel as the Resolution.

You can save images without alpha channels at 16 bits/pixel, but this option may introduce banding in fine gradients. However, if the file has an alpha channel and 16 bits/pixel is selected, the alpha channel will not be saved.

b. Click OK.

Photoshop saves the new file to the selected destination.

Optional File Modifications

Some images require additional steps to prepare them for importing.

Changing the Color Space

Files should be saved with using the RGB color space. You may receive files using CMYK, Grayscale or Index color spaces.

- CMYK is a subtractive color space designed for print applications. Although you can save CMYK files in many of the formats that Avid Xpress DV supports, these files will import with incorrect colors.

- Grayscale images only contain luminance information. Though basic Grayscale images will import into Avid Xpress DV, Grayscale images with alpha channels will only import if saved as a Photoshop file.

- Index color images contain only a limited number of colors, usually only 256 or fewer distinct colors. Photoshop can only perform limited operations on Index color images. These images will not import correctly into Avid Xpress DV.

Be sure to convert all files to RGB color before importing into Avid Xpress DV.

To change the color space:

■ Choose Image > Mode > RGB Color.

Cropping Very Wide or Very Tall Images

Occasionally you will encounter images with aspect ratios dramatically different from the desired 4x3 or 16x9 video aspect ratios. Though in some instances you will be able to crop the image to fit it within video's aspect ratio, some times you need to maintain the full width or height of the image.

This can be accomplished using the Crop tool. Photoshop will fill the region around the image with a color that you specify. All that is required is a little advance setup.

Preparing for Cropping

1. Open the image in Photoshop.

2. Click on the Background Color button in the Tool palette.

The Background Color Picker appears.

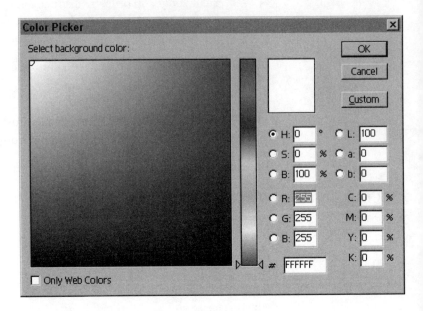

3. Select the color you want Photoshop to use for the area around the image.

   Black is the most commonly used color, but you can choose another one, if desired.

 If you click on the image when the Color Picker is open, the color you click on will be sampled and selected.

4. Click OK to close the Color Picker.

5. Reduce the size of the image and its window until it takes up no more than one fourth available space in the Photoshop window.

   This can be accomplished from the keyboard by repeatedly pressing Control+Alt+– (Windows) or Command+Option+– (Macintosh) until the desired size is reached.

6. Resize the window by dragging from any edge (Windows) or from the bottom right corner (Macintosh) until it is at least twice as large as it was previously.

7. Select the Crop tool and confirm that the proper frame size is listed in the Crop options.

8. Draw an initial crop region around a portion of the image.

9. Click on one of the handles, hold the Alt key (Windows) or Option key (Macintosh) downand resize the crop rectangle until it spills over into the area around the image.

   The Alt (Windows) or Option (Macintosh) modifier instructs Photoshop to resize the crop window from the center.

10. Adjust the position and size of the crop region until you have enclosed all of the image you need to retain and the image is centered within the crop region.

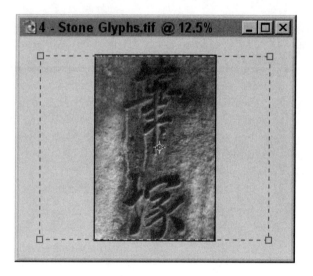

11. Press the Enter key to perform the crop.

The image is cropped to the size you specified in the Crop options and the region around the image is filled with the color you specified.

Sizing an Image to Safe Action

Certain images must be completely visible on video. If the source image has been tightly cropped for print or web use, an important portion of the image may reside outside of Safe Action. In these instances you should resize the image so the entire image fits within Safe Action and then add a neutral color around the image so it is properly sized for import.

To size an image to Safe Action:

1. Select the Crop tool.

2. Set the crop size to one of the Safe Action sizes listed in the following table.

Format	Desired Final Size	Safe Action Size	14x9 Safe Size[†]
NTSC 4x3	640 x 480	576 x 432	not applicable
NTSC 16x9	853 x 480	768 x 432	not applicable
PAL 4x3	768 x 576	698 x 518	not applicable
PAL 16x9	1024 x 576	922 x 518	892 x 518

[†] *14x9 Safe Size refers to the 14x9 Safe Area required by many European broadcasters when delivering shows with a 16x9 aspect ratio. In these*

instances, the 14x9 Safe Size should be used instead of the traditional Safe Action size.

3. Crop the image as desired.

4. Click on the Background Color button in the Tool palette.

   The Background Color Picker appears.

5. Select the color you want Photoshop to use for the area around the image.

   Black is the most commonly used color, but you can choose another one, if desired.

   If you click on the image with the Color Picker open, the color you click on will be sampled and selected.

6. Click OK to close the Color Picker.

7. Choose Image > Canvas Size

   The Canvas Size dialog opens.

8. Enter the final image size desired.

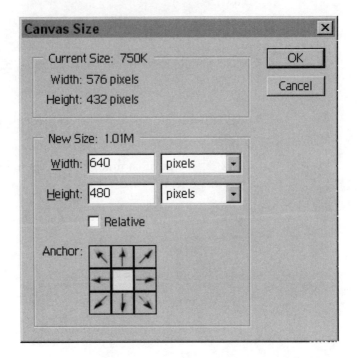

9. Click OK to close the Canvas Size dialog and fill the area around the image with the selected background color.

Review Questions

1. What are the requirements for an image that will be imported into Avid Xpress DV? *(See "Criteria for Import" on page 1-2.)*

2. How can you determine the size, color mode, and resolution of an image? *(See "Determining the Image Size and Color Mode" on page 1-6.)*

3. How is the Adobe Photoshop Crop Tool helpful in preparing still graphics you plan to import into Avid Xpress DV? *(See "Cropping the Image to the Proper Size" on page 1-7.)*

Exercise 1

Preparing Still Graphics

In this exercise, you'll prepare several graphic stills for import into Avid Xpress DV. Refer to Module 1 for the exact steps.

Preparing the Files

1. Launch Adobe Photoshop.

2. Open, crop, and save all of the images in the **Graphics\Exercise 1** folder so they are ready to import into Avid Xpress DV.

   The following table lists the files you need to convert and whether any special procedures are required.

File Name	Special Procedure Required
1-Gold Pavilion.tif	Straighten image, save as a 4x3 image
2-Waterskiier.tif	Save as a 4x3 image
3-Tiger.tif	Check color space, save as a 16x9 image
4-Stone Glyphs.tif	Keep all of the image within safe action, save as 4x3 image
5-Fishing Village.tif	Save as a 16x9 image
6-Fall Leaves.tif	Save as a 4x3 image
7-Mesh Grids.tif	Save both a 4x3 and a 16x9 version
8-Battered Steel.tif	Save as a 4x3 image
9-Produce.tif	Save as a 16x9 image

3. Be sure to append -640, -850, -768 or -1024 to the name of each file.

Images with a 4x3 aspect ratio should be appended with either -640 or -768. Images with a 16x9 aspect ratio should be appended with either -850 or -1024.

Module 2

Importing and Exporting Still Graphics

In Avid Xpress DV you can import a wide range of file types to satisfy an equally wide range of editing needs. However, any still graphic you wish to import should meet the criteria we mentioned in the previous module. (See "Criteria for Import" on page 1-2.)

When Avid Xpress DV imports a file, it creates any necessary media files and stores them on a hard drive.

Objectives

After you complete this module, you will be able to:

- Import graphic stills into a Avid Xpress DV project
- Understand the options associated with the import process
- Export frames from Avid Xpress DV

Supported File Types

Avid Xpress DV supports twenty four still graphic file formats. The most common formats are TIFF, PICT and Photoshop. The following table lists the most commonly used file types. The table also lists the format's file extension, whether an alpha channel is supported, and any applicable comments.

 Even though Avid Xpress DV does not require a extension in order to recognize a file, extensions should be used to maintain compatibility across programs and platforms.

Format	Extension	Alpha?	Comments
Alias	.als	No	Alpha must be saved as a separate file.
BMP	.bmp	No	
Chyron	.chr	Yes	Images must be saved as a frame store file.
JPEG	.jpg	No	CMYK images are not supported.
Photoshop	.psd	Yes	Grayscale, CMYK, Lab images, and files with more than four channels are not supported.
PICT	.pct	Yes	
PNG	.png	Yes	
Softimage	.pic	Yes	
Targa	.tga	Yes	
TIFF	.tif	Yes	Supported: RGB images, Grayscale images, TIFF files with layers (created with Photoshop 6 or later)
			Unsupported: CMYK images, files with more than four channels, and Group 3 Fax files

Importing Still Graphic Files

1. Select the bin where you want to store the imported files.

2. Choose File > Import.

   The import dialog box appears.

Windows

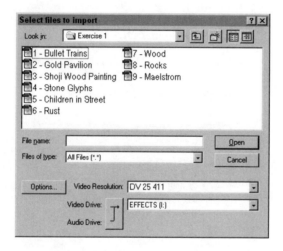

Macintosh

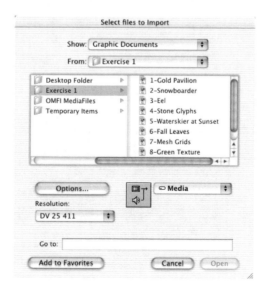

3. Navigate to the folder where the import elements are stored.

4. Select the file(s) to import.

   (Windows) To select multiple files: use the Control or Shift keys to select multiple files at once. The Control key allows you to select discontiguous files while the Shift key allows you to select contiguous files.

   (Macintosh) To select multiple files: use the Shift key to select multiple files at once.

5. Choose the Media Drive.

6. Click the Options button.

   The Import Settings dialog box opens.

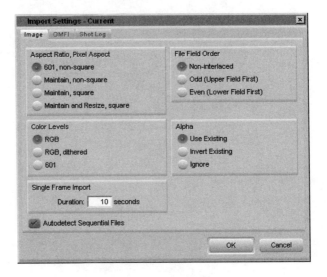

7. Use the following section to help you set the various import options.

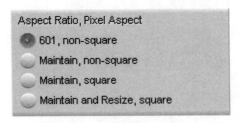

- **601, non-square** —This is the system default. This option assumes the file is properly sized for import and leaves the image alone. If the image is not properly sized, this option forces the image to fit the entire video frame and will distort images with non-television aspect ratios.

- **Maintain, non-square** — (NTSC only) This option is designed to be used with full frame non-square NTSC images imported into an NTSC DV project. The full NTSC frame has a size of 720 x 486 (as opposed to the 720 x 480 frame size of NTSC DV). The top four lines and bottom two lines of the 720 x 486 frame are removed from the image. This conforms to the SMPTE specification for NTSC DV frames.

- **Maintain, square** — This option is designed to be used with images that are smaller than the video frame size and cannot be resized. It does not attempt to resize the image, but compensates for the square pixels, centers it within the video frame and adds video black around the image. This option is designed to make it easy to bring in small graphics, such as web-originated art, into Xpress DV.

- **Maintain and Resize, square** — This option assumes an incorrect image size. It letterboxes the image with video black and resizes it to fit either the 720 pixel width (for wide images) or the 480 (NTSC) or 576 (PAL) height (for tall images). It also assumes the import file has square pixels and compensates accordingly.

If the graphic has an alpha channel and one of the three Maintain options is chosen, the system will key out the area around the graphic instead of adding video black.

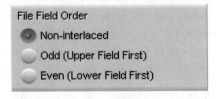

- Allows you to set the field ordering of the import file. Should be set to Non-interlaced when importing still graphics.

  The other two field order options are used when importing animations and video. We'll discuss this option further in Module 8.

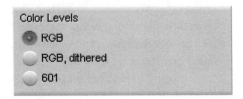

- **RGB** — Designed to be used with traditionally created computer images. The blackest black in the graphic will be assigned the value of video black and the whitest white will be assigned the value of video white.

  This option should be chosen for graphics and animations created in third party programs.

- **RGB, dithered** — Assigns values identically to RGB. Select this option if you are importing a graphic with a fine gradient. Due to the limitations of 8-bit 4:2:2 video encoding, banding is possible in fine gradients. This option adds a slight amount of noise to the gradient and masks the banding inherent in digital video.

- **601** — Use this option if the graphic was created specifically to use the extended signal range available in the ITU-R BT.601 video standard.

  We will discuss the 601 option in greater detail in Module 8.

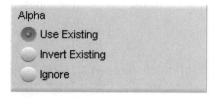

- **Use Existing** — Applies only to images that have an alpha channel; the setting has no effect on images that don't have an alpha channel.

- **Invert Existing** — Inverts the black and white areas in an alpha channel.

- **Ignore** — If this option is selected, the system disregards the alpha channel and imports only the RGB portion of the image.

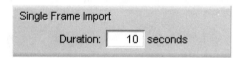

- Allows you to specify the duration in seconds for still graphics.

  The duration chosen does not impact the storage space used by the graphic. It only affects the duration of the graphic in the bin.

8. When you are satisfied with the Import Settings, click OK to return to the Import dialog.

9. Click OK to begin the import process.

Drag-and-Drop Method

Another way to import a file is to drag it directly from its location on disk to the desired bin.

1. Open the bin you want to store the graphic in.

2. Using Windows Explorer (Windows) or the Finder (Macintosh), navigate to the folder that contains the graphics.

3. Drag the file or files you wish to import from the folder to the bin.

The file will be imported using the current Import setting.

 Although this method can save you time, you must be careful that the Import settings are appropriate for the file you are importing.

Changing the Duration of an Imported Still

The Import settings allow you to specify an import duration in seconds. However, in certain situations, such as with pre-timed credit cards, you may need a duration in frames. You can change the duration using the Console prior to import. The duration you enter will override the duration set in the Import Settings dialog box.

1. Open the Console by choosing Tools > Console.

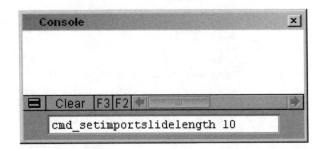

2. Click in the lower area of the Console window and type the following command:

cmd_setimportslidelength XX

Replace XX with duration, in frames, you want the graphic to have.

3. Press the Return key.

This changes the length for all imported graphic stills and titles until you enter a new value or quit the program. It does not affect the length of graphics or titles you already imported.

Exporting Still Frames from Avid Xpress DV

You can export still frames using any of the file formats available for import.

1. Load the clip or sequence containing the frame you wish to export into the Source or Record monitor.

2. Park on the desired frame and make sure the appropriate track is monitored.

3. Choose File > Export.

   The Export dialog box opens.

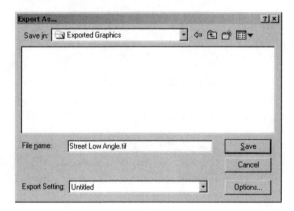

At the bottom of the Export dialog, a pop-up menu allows you to choose from a list of Export settings. Xpress DV creates three Export settings when you create a user, but you can create additional settings.

4. Click the Options button to open the Export Settings dialog box.

   The Export Settings dialog box opens.

5. If necessary, choose Graphic from the Export As pop-up menu.

The Export as Graphic options appear.

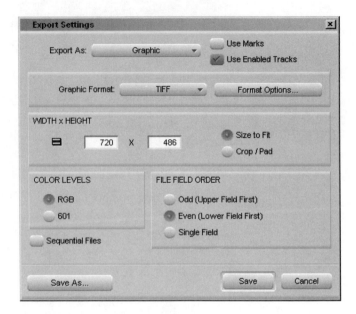

6. Use the following section to help you set the various export options.

- **Use Marks** — If set, the Avid Xpress DV exports the frame at the IN point or, in the absence of an IN point, at the blue position indicator. If not set, the Avid Xpress DV exports the first frame of the clip.

- **Use Enabled Tracks** — This option controls which track(s) are exported in a multilayer sequence.

  - If Use Enabled Tracks is deselected, the sequence will export the sequence from the highest monitored track.

  - If Use Enabled Tracks is selected, the sequence will export the sequence from the highest active track.

  This option is designed to allow an editor to select a large number of audio tracks and export them in a group. It should be disabled when exporting graphics and video only.

- **Graphic Format** — Choose the format you wish to export to from the pop-up menu. Most graphic exports will use either TIFF or PICT.

- **Format Options** — This button displays the options available for the chosen graphic format.

  If TIFF was the chosen format and Format Options were chosen, the following dialog would appear.

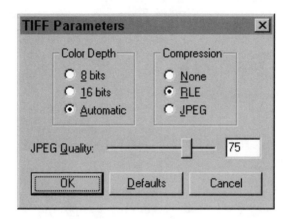

The displayed options, Automatic Color Depth and RLE Compression are the preferred options.

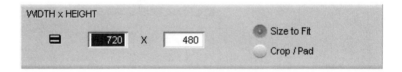

- **Width, Height** — Enter the size required or choose one from the Fast menu to the left. Refer to the table below for the recommended sizes.

Format	4x3 Aspect Ratio Square Pixel	16x9 Aspect Ratio Square Pixel	Native Size Non-Square Pixel
NTSC	640 x 480	853 x 480	720 x 480
NTSC (non-DV)	648 x 486	864 x 486	720 x 486
PAL	768 x 576	1024 x 576	720 x 576

- Use a Square Pixel size when exporting a graphic that will be used for print or the web.

- Use the Native Size when exporting a graphic for use in After Effects or other compositing program.

- Use the Native Size when exporting a graphic that will be retouched and reimported into Avid Xpress DV.

- **Scale to Fit** or **Crop / Pad** — Determines how the image is fit into the export size.

  - Use Scale to Fit for all instances except when exporting a still to the non-DV NTSC frame sizes.

  - Use Crop / Pad when exporting a still for use in an a standard NTSC (non-DV) project.

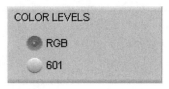

- RGB should be chosen for most graphic exports, especially when a frame is exported for use in print or on the web.

  The 601 option is most commonly used when exporting frames with specular highlights that will be retouched and reimported into Avid Xpress DV. We will discuss the 601 option in detail in Module 8.

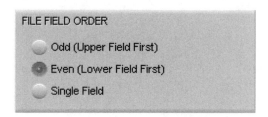

- The Single Field option exports only one of the two video fields and is usually the best option when exporting still graphics.

- The other two options will export both video fields and is used primarily when exporting video clips.

  We will discuss this option in detail in Module 8.

7. Deselect the Sequential Files option.

8. Click on the Save As... button and name this setting.

   Saving a setting allows you to easily switch between different export configurations. Use a name that makes the options easy to identify. For example, *RGB TIFF Graphic.*

9. Navigate to the location you wish to save the graphic to.

10. Enter a name for the graphic.

Don't use non-alphanumeric characters, such as \ / | * ? : < > in the file name. These characters are not allowed in filenames on Windows or Unix systems.

11. Click OK to save the graphic.

Avid Xpress DV automatically adds a three-character extension to the end of the file name. This extension is required if the file is intended to be used on a Windows or Unix system. The extension is not required, but recommended, if you are only using the file on the Macintosh.

Review Questions

1. What should the Aspect Ratio, Pixel Aspect option be set to when importing images that are properly sized for import? *(See "Aspect Ratio, Pixel Aspect" on page 2-5")*

2. What should the Aspect Ratio, Pixel Aspect option be set to when importing NTSC full frame (non-DV) images? *(See "Aspect Ratio, Pixel Aspect" on page 2-5")*

3. What is the correct frame size to use when exporting a 4x3 image for use in print or on the web? *(See "Width, Height" on page 2-11)*

Exercise 2

Importing Still Graphics

In this exercise, you'll import the still graphics you prepared in the previous exercise. Refer to Module 2 for the exact steps.

Importing the Files

1. Launch Avid Xpress DV.

2. Open the Creating Graphics project.

3. Create a new bin and name it "Imports"

4. Import all of the files you cropped in the previous exercise.

   Use the following Import settings:

   - Aspect Ratio, Pixel Aspect: 601, non-square

   - File Field Order: Non-interlaced

   - Color Levels: RGB

   - Alpha: Ignore

   - Duration: 10 seconds

5. Load each imported graphic into the Source monitor and confirm that the graphic appears to be properly cropped and sized.

   Remember that four images, 3-Tiger.tif, 5-Fishing Village.tif, 7-Mesh Grids.tif, and 9-Produce.tif, were sized to a 16x9 frame. To see them properly you will need to switch the Composer window to 16x9 mode.

a. (Windows) Right-click on the Composer window and select **16x9 Video** from the pop-up menu.

(Macintosh) Hold the Control and Shift keys down, click on the Composer window and select **16x9 Video** from the pop-up menu.

b. After viewing the 16x9 images, deselect **16x9 Video** from the pop-up menu to return to the Composer window to 4x3.

(Macintosh) If you purchase and connect a two-button mouse to an OS X system, you can use Right-click instead of Control-Shift-click to display the contextual menu.

6. If any of the files do not appear to be properly cropped or sized, open the source image in Photoshop and crop it again.

Module 3

Creating Alpha Channels

You create an alpha channel for an image using a third party package such as Adobe Photoshop. You can then import the image and alpha channel into Avid Xpress DV for advanced matte key effects.

Objectives

After you complete this module, you will be able to:

- Create alpha channels in Adobe Photoshop using the Magic Wand tool

- Clean up and modify alpha channels using Quick Mask

- Create alpha channels using Quick Mask

Creating Alpha Channels with Adobe Photoshop

You can use Adobe Photoshop to create alpha channels, or mattes for images that you plan to use in Avid Xpress DV.

An image is stored using channels of information. A graphic file usually has three channels, one for each of the primary colors (red, green, and blue). Photoshop allows you to view these channels individually or merged together to form the full color image.

An alpha channel is a fourth channel that defines where the RGB channels are visible and where they are transparent. The alpha channel can be created from a selection of the RGB channels or created independently of the RGB channels.

This module will introduce two techniques that can be used to create an alpha channel.

- **Magic Wand Tool** — This tool allows you to create an alpha channel by selecting regions of similarly colored pixels.

  This tool is most effective when the image has a solid color background.

- **Quick Mask Mode** — Quick Mask mode allows you to clean up a selection or create a selection from scratch.

  This tool is most effective when the image has a complex background.

Using the Channels Palette

The Channels palette lists all the channels for the current image and provides access to the individual channels for editing or viewing.

To open the Channels palette:

■ Choose Window > Show Channels.

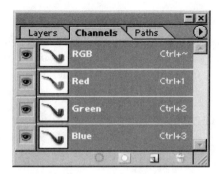

The channel names are listed next to corresponding thumbnails. Use the Channels palette to select the channels you are viewing and editing.

• Click on the Eye icon to view or hide a channel.

Click on the Eye icon next to the RGB "channel" to view or hide the R, G, and B channels.

• Click on the channel name to select a channel for editing.

Click on the RGB "channel" to select the Red, Green, and Blue channels.

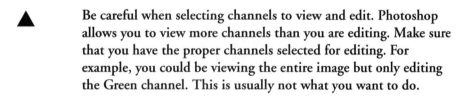 Be careful when selecting channels to view and edit. Photoshop allows you to view more channels than you are editing. Make sure that you have the proper channels selected for editing. For example, you could be viewing the entire image but only editing the Green channel. This is usually not what you want to do.

Using the Magic Wand Tool

The Magic Wand Tool creates a selection by finding pixels in an image that have similar color values. This allows you to select a large area, such as a blue sky by clicking on a portion of the sky. The range of colors selected can be adjusted via the Tolerance option.

Making the Initial Selection

1. Open the file you wish to create an alpha channel for.

2. If necessary, crop and resize the image so it is the proper size for import.

   It is often easier to set the image size before creating the alpha channel than it is to adjust the size afterward.

3. Select the Magic Wand tool by clicking on it in the Tool Palette or by typing W on the keyboard.

4. Select Anti-Alias in the Magic Wand options bar.

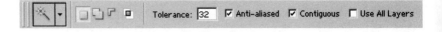

   Anti-aliasing smooths the jagged edges of a selection by blending the transition between the edge pixels and the background. It does not affect any pixels within the selection, just those on the edge.

5. Set the Tolerance to 32.

This is a good starting point. You may need to adjust this level for different images. A smaller tolerance selects only pixels that are similar in color to the one you click on; a larger tolerance selects a wider range of colors.

6. Click in the foreground or the background, depending on which area contains uniform color.

Adobe Photoshop selects a region made up of adjacent pixels that fall within the tolerance range.

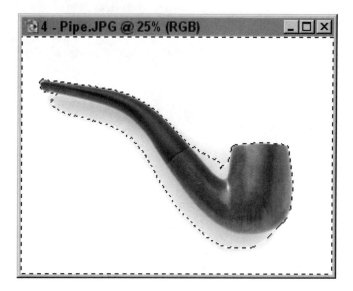

Adding Areas to the Selection

If the background is uneven or contains shadows, the magic wand may not select all of the background. In these instances you can add to the selection.

- With the Magic Wand Tool active, hold down the Shift key and click inside an area that was not previously selected.

This method works well when the image contains shadows or backgrounds with more than one color. For best results, click on a pixel in the middle of the region you wish to add. In some instances you may wish to increase the tolerance before you Shift+click additional pixels.

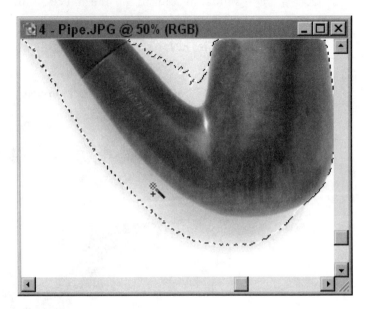

- Choose Similar from the Select menu to select nonadjacent pixels with a similar color range.

  This method is best when the foreground has holes or divides the background, such as a window pane.

Removing Areas from the Selection

Sometimes the Magic Wand selects too many pixels. Photoshop allows you to use the Magic Wand to remove areas from a selection.

- With the Magic Wand tool active, hold the Alt key (Windows) or Option key (Macintosh) and click on a pixel within a selected area to subtract that color from the selection.

  This method is useful when you over select a region and want to remove part of the selection.

  You may find it helpful to reduce the tolerance before removing an area from a selection.

Choking the Selection

The Magic Wand Tool is good for roughing out the mask, but the edges may need additional attention. Because the Magic Wand selects all pixels within a given tonal range, it selects all of the background up to the edge of the object you are keying. If you zoom in on the edge of the image you see that the selection is right at the edge of the image.

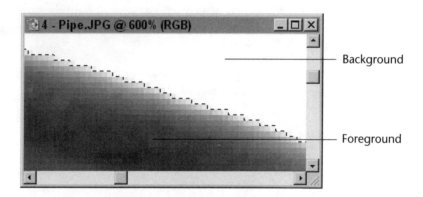

Background

Foreground

Remember that we enabled Anti-aliasing. Anti-aliasing introduces a two pixel wide fall off from opacity to transparency at the edge. The following illustration shows this two-pixel-wide area. Notice that this area includes not only foreground pixels, but background pixels as well.

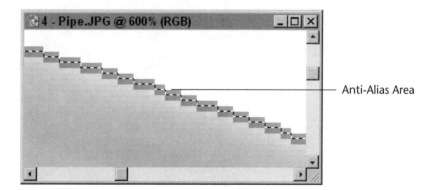

Anti-Alias Area

If you leave the selection alone, the foreground image will have faint line of the background color (white in this example) along the edge of the image, which you will see when you composite the graphic in Avid

Xpress DV. You need to *choke* the selection so the anti-aliased region includes only pixels of the object and not the background.

You use either Expand or Contract to accomplish this task. The command you choose depends upon whether the background or the foreground is selected. You can tell which is selected by looking at the edge of the graphic.

- If there is a dotted line around both the foreground and the edge of the frame, then the background is selected and you should choose Expand.

- If the dotted line is only around the object, then the foreground is selected and you should choose Contract.

1. Refer to the rules above and select either Select > Modify > Expand or Select > Modify > Contract.

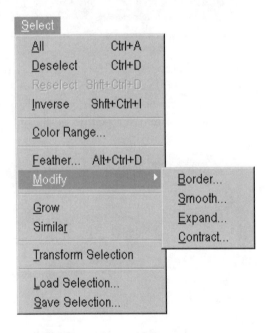

2. In the dialog box, enter a value of 1 pixel. Click OK.

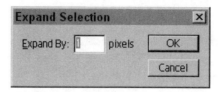

The selection is choked into the foreground.

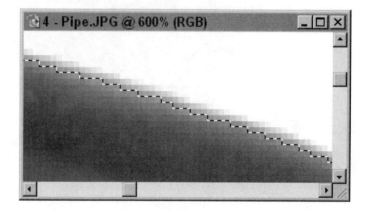

Saving the Selection as an Alpha Channel

The next step is to save the selection as an alpha channel.

■ Click on the Save Selection button at the bottom of the Channels palette.

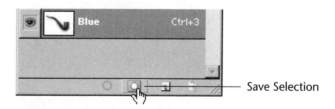

An alpha channel is created from the selection and listed in the Channels palette.

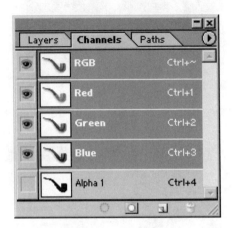

 The file should only have one alpha channel. If you accidentally create two alpha channels, delete one of them by dragging it to the Trash button in the lower right hand corner of the Channels palette.

Defining Transparency with an Alpha Channel

Let's look closer at the alpha channel. An alpha channel is a gray scale channel that defines what areas of the RGB will be opaque and which will be transparent.

In Photoshop, when an alpha channel is created from a selection the selected region is assumed to be the foreground and defined as opaque. Unselected areas are assumed to be background and defined as transparent.

Therefore, the alpha channel created from our selection looks like the following illustration.

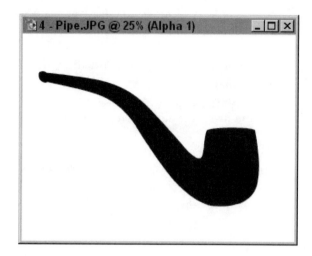

Traditional video alpha channels are defined so that white represents fully opaque areas and black represents fully transparent areas. Gray values represent a degree of transparency.

Notice that the alpha channel created when we select the background is not created using the traditional definition, but is instead inverted. If we wanted this alpha channel to be traditionally defined, we should invert the alpha channel.

To Invert an Alpha Channel

1. Click on the alpha channel in the Channels palette to activate it and deactivate all other channels.

2. Clear any active selection by choosing Select > Deselect or by typing Control+D (Windows) or Command+D (Macintosh).

3. Select Image > Adjust > Invert or type Control+I (Windows) or Command+I (Macintosh).

Alpha Channels and Avid Xpress DV

Avid Xpress DV uses a different alpha channel definition, one derived from film. In Avid Xpress DV *black* represents fully opaque areas and *white* represents fully transparent areas.

Even though Avid Xpress DV uses this film-based definition internally, alpha channels can still be created with the traditional definition (white represents opaque, black represents transparent) because Avid Xpress DV can invert the alpha channel during import.

The key is to be consistent. We recommend that you create all of your alpha channels using the traditional definition. The last thing you want when importing graphics into Avid Xpress DV is to have some defined one way and others defined the other way.

Saving the File

Now that the alpha channel is created, the file is ready to be saved.

1. Choose File > Save As to save the new image and alpha channel.

   As mentioned in the previous module, it is always preferable to use Save As and create a new file instead of saving over the original. This way you can always go back to the original file, if necessary.

2. Append the file name to indicate that the file is properly sized for import.

   You might also want to indicate that the image has an alpha channel, for example 640A or -768A.

3. If necessary, navigate to the folder you wish to save the files in.

4. Choose TIFF from the list of formats in the Format pop-up menu.

5. Click Save.

6. Choose LZW for the compression in the TIFF Options dialog box and click OK.

   Photoshop saves the new file to the selected destination.

Using Quick Mask Mode

The Magic Wand tool is a good tool to rough out an alpha channel, but for many images it alone cannot provide the quality needed. Photoshop offers a mode, called Quick Mask, that allows you to use Photoshop's painting tools to clean up the edges of the selection.

Quick Mask can also be used by itself to create an alpha channel from scratch.

Using Quick Mask to Clean up a Selection

The most common use of Quick Mask is to clean up a selection created by the Magic Wand and/or other selection tools.

Creating the Initial Selection and Entering Quick Mask

1. Open the image you need to create an alpha channel for.

2. Crop and size the image for import.

3. Use the Magic Wand tool to rough out a selection.

   Try to get as clean a selection as possible, but don't worry about every problem at the edges. You'll clean these up using Quick Mask

4. Click the Quick Mask button towards the bottom of the Tool palette.

The image display changes. The selection is now displayed as an editable color overlay. Photoshop has created a temporary alpha channel and activated it for editing. Both the temporary channel and the RGB channels are displayed.

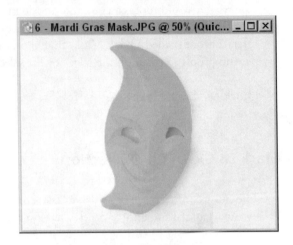

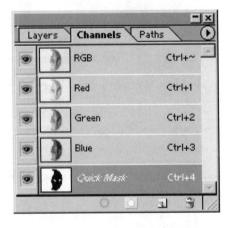

 An alpha channel is always displayed as a color overlay if it and the RGB channels are displayed simultaneously.

Configuring the Quick Mask

By default, the editable overlay is assigned the color of red and given a 50% opacity. This default option is designed to mimic the rubylith method used in traditional pre-press production. This color may not work for all images, especially those with red at the edges. You can change the color and the way the Quick Mask is displayed.

1. Double-click the Quick Mask button.

   The Quick Mask options dialog box opens.

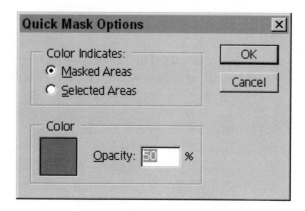

2. Adjust the Quick Mask using one or more of the following options.

   - Click on the Color box to open the Color Picker and select a different overlay color.

   - Change the Opacity percentage.

     - Higher values make the overlay more opaque.

     - Lower values make the overlay more transparent.

   - Swap the location of the color overlay by changing the Color Indicates option.

     - Masked Areas — The color overlay is applied to all areas that are not selected. If the background was selected, the color overlay will cover the foreground.

     - Selected Areas — The color overlay is applied to all selected areas. If the background was selected, the color overlay will cover the background.

   When cleaning up the edges of an object, you may find it helpful to switch the color overlay back and forth. This is an especially good way to check whether you are inadvertently over correcting on an edge and adding or removing too much information.

It is not necessary to open the Quick Mask Options to switch the color overlay. Alt+click (Windows) or Option+click (Macintosh) the Quick Mask button to switch the overlay.

Cleaning up the Selection Edge

The edge is cleaned up in Quick Mask by using one of the paint tools to either add to or remove from the color overlay. Though any painting tool can be used, the best tool to use is the Paintbrush.

1. Select the Paintbrush tool by clicking on the Paintbrush icon in the Tool palette or by typing B on the keyboard.

2. Open the Brush selector in the Brush options bar and select one of the brushes from the first group.

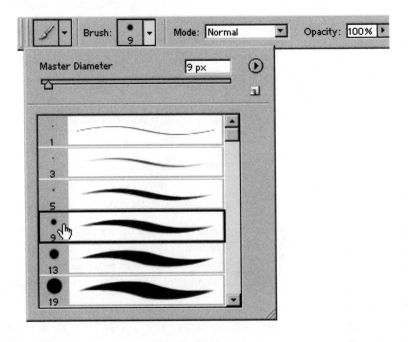

The brushes in the first group have an anti-aliased edge that closely matches that of the Magic Wand. Brushes in the other groups have a much wider anti-alias area and, as a result, cleanup performed using them will not match the other edges of the selection.

3. Reset the Foreground and Background colors to black and white by clicking on the Reset Colors button or by typing D on the keyboard.

4. Use the Paintbrush to touch up the edges.

- When the foreground is set to black, the paintbrush adds to the mask.

- When the foreground is set to white, the paintbrush subtracts from the mask.

- Switch the foreground between black and white by pressing the X key on the keyboard.

  The X key switches the foreground and background colors. Since you reset the foreground to black and the background to white, the X key switches the foreground between black and white.

- Use the square bracket ([,])keys to decrease or increase the brush size.

5. Continue touching up the mask until you are satisfied with it.

The following key commands can help you view and navigate around the image:

- Alt+click (Windows) or Option+click (Macintosh) the Quick Mask mode button to switch the overlay.

- Type Control++ (Windows) or Command++ (Macintosh) to zoom in.

- Type Control+− (Windows) or Command+− (Macintosh) to zoom out.

- Hold the Space bar down and drag the image with the mouse to navigate around the image.

6. Once you are satisfied with the mask, click the Standard Mode button to exit Quick Mask mode.

The mask shape is replaced with a selection.

- If there is a dotted line around both the foreground and the edge of the frame, then the background is selected and you should choose Expand.

- If the dotted line is only around the object, then the foreground is selected and you should choose Contract.

7. Choose Select > Modify > Expand.

If the dotted line is only around the object, then choose Select > Modify > Contract, instead.

8. In the dialog box, enter a value of 1 pixel. Click OK.

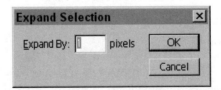

The selection is choked into the foreground.

9. Click on the Save Selection button at the bottom of the Channels palette.

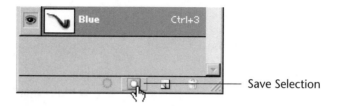

Save Selection

An alpha channel is created from the selection and listed in the Channels palette.

Inverting the Alpha Channel (Optional)

Remember that you should create all alpha channels so that opacity and transparency are always represented in the same way. If the alpha channel you created is opposite from the method you decided to standardize on, you need to invert it before saving.

1. Click on the alpha channel in the Channels palette to activate it and deactivate all other channels.

2. Clear any active selection by choosing Select > Deselect or by typing Control+D (Windows) or Command+D (Macintosh).

3. Select Image > Adjust > Invert or type Control+I (Windows) or Command+I (Macintosh).

Saving the File

Now that the alpha channel is created, the file is ready to be saved.

1. Choose File > Save As to save the new image and alpha channel.

As mentioned in the previous module, it is always preferable to use Save As and create a new file instead of saving over the original. This way you can always go back to the original file, if necessary.

2. Append the file name to indicate that the file is properly sized for import

3. If necessary, navigate to the folder you wish to save the files in.

4. Choose TIFF from the list of formats in the Format pop-up menu.

5. Click Save.

6. Choose LZW for the compression in the TIFF Options dialog box and click OK.

   Photoshop saves the new file to the selected destination.

Painting a Mask from Scratch

Sometimes it is difficult or impossible to even roughly isolate the foreground from the background using the selection tools. In these instances, you can create the mask from scratch using Quick Mask mode:

1. Open the image and crop and size it for import.

2. Click the Quick Mask button towards the bottom of the Tool palette.

3. Select the Paintbrush tool by clicking on the Paintbrush icon in the Tool palette or by typing B on the keyboard.

4. Open the Brush selector in the Brush options bar and select one of the brushes from the top row.

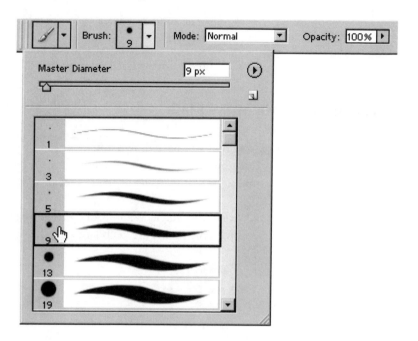

5. Reset the Foreground and Background colors to black and white by clicking on the Reset Colors button or by typing D on the keyboard.

6. With short, smooth strokes, paint along the *inside edge* of the foreground object.

   • When the foreground is set to black, the paintbrush adds to the mask.

   • When the foreground is set to white, the paintbrush subtracts from the mask.

- Switch the foreground between black and white by clicking the X key on the keyboard.

- Use the square bracket ([,])keys to decrease or increase the brush size.

7. Continue painting until you have a closed shape.

Filling the Inside of the Mask

Now that you have drawn a mask around the entire edge of the foreground element, you need to fill the interior so that you have a solid mask. To fill the inside of the shape:

1. Select the Magic Wand tool by clicking on it in the Tool Palette or by typing W on the keyboard.

2. Click inside the closed shape.

   The inside of the object, up to the Quick Mask boundary, becomes selected. If the Magic Wand selected both the inside and the outside of the shape, you did not close the outline.

   a. Type Control+D (Windows) or Command+D (Macintosh) to clear the selection.

   b. Select the Paintbrush tool and close the shape where necessary.

   c. Reselect the Magic Wand tool and click inside the shape.

3. Choose Select > Modify > Expand.

   The selection needs to be expanded into the outline shape you drew. If the selection is not expanded, there will be a thin area at the edge of the Magic Wand selection that will not be filled in. This is due to the anti-aliasing of the Paintbrush and Magic Wand tools.

4. In the dialog box, enter 2 pixels and click OK.

   The selection expands by two pixels.

5. Choose Edit > Fill.

6. Choose Black from the Use pop-up menu.

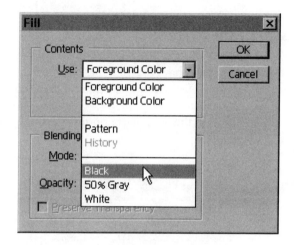

The interior of your outline is filled.

7. Inspect and, if necessary, clean up the mask.

8. Once you are satisfied with the mask, click the Standard Mode button to exit Quick Mask mode.

The mask shape is replaced with a selection.

9. Choose Select > Modify > Expand.

If the dotted line is only around the object, then choose Select > Modify > Contract, instead.

10. In the dialog box, enter a value of 1 pixel. Click OK.

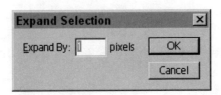

The selection is choked into the foreground.

11. Click on the Save Selection button at the bottom of the Channels palette.

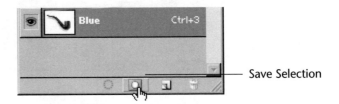

An alpha channel is created from the selection and listed in the Channels palette.

Inverting the Alpha Channel (Optional)

Remember that you should create all alpha channels so that opacity and transparency are always represented in the same way. If the alpha channel you created is opposite from the method you decided to standardize on, you need to invert it before saving.

1. Click on the alpha channel in the Channels palette to activate it and deactivate all other channels.

2. Clear any active selection by choosing Select > Deselect or by typing Control+D (Windows) or Command+D (Macintosh).

3. Select Image > Adjust > Invert or type Control+I (Windows) or Command+I (Macintosh).

Saving the File

Now that the alpha channel is created, the file is ready to be saved.

1. Choose File > Save As to save the new image and alpha channel.

   As mentioned in the previous module, it is always preferable to use Save As and create a new file instead of saving over the original. This way you can always go back to the original file, if necessary.

2. Append the file name to indicate that the file is properly sized for import

3. If necessary, navigate to the folder you wish to save the files in.

4. Choose TIFF from the list of formats in the Format pop-up menu.

5. Click Save.

6. Choose LZW for the compression in the TIFF Options dialog box and click OK.

   Photoshop saves the new file to the selected destination.

Touching Up a Previously Saved Alpha Channel

Sometimes you need to touch up an alpha channel in a file that you already saved. The alpha channel can be directly edited and viewed similarly to the Quick Mask.

1. Open the image containing the alpha channel that needs touching up

2. Click on the alpha channel in the Channels palette to view it and activate it for editing.

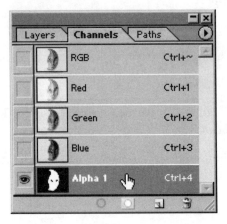

3. Click on the Eye next to the RGB "channel" to view the RGB channels in addition to the alpha channel.

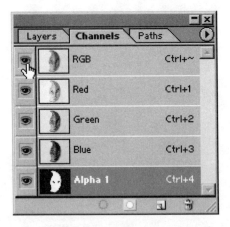

The alpha channel is now displayed in the image window as an editable color overlay. Black areas in the alpha are represented by the overlay.

4. Use the Paintbrush to touch up the alpha channel.

   - Use the D key to reset the Foreground and Background colors to black and white, respectively.

   - Use the X key to switch the foreground color between black and white.

5. When you have satisfactorily touched up the alpha channel, select File > Save to save the changes.

Review Questions

1. What is an alpha channel? *(See "Creating Alpha Channels with Adobe Photoshop" on page 3-2.)*

2. In Avid Xpress DV, which part of the alpha channel is transparent and which part is opaque? *(See "Defining Transparency with an Alpha Channel" on page 3-10.)*

3. When cutting a mask, in what situations is it best to use the Magic Wand Tool? The Quick Mask mode? *(See "Creating Alpha Channels with Adobe Photoshop" on page 3-2.)*

4. What keyboard commands are useful when editing a selection in Quick Mask mode? *(See "Cleaning up the Selection Edge" on page 3-16.)*

Exercise 3

Creating Alpha Channels

You are going to create alpha channels for several images, which you will then import into Avid Xpress DV. Like the graphic stills you cropped and sized in Exercise 1, the images should meet the standard set of criteria for Avid Xpress DV import.

Use the Magic Wand tool and Quick Mask mode to create an alpha channel for each of the images in the **Graphics\Exercise 3** folder. The final alpha channels should all use the traditional designation for opacity and transparency (white for opaque areas, black for transparent areas).

Creating the Alpha Channels

1. Launch Adobe Photoshop.

2. Open and crop each image so it is properly sized for import into Avid Xpress DV.

3. Use the Magic Wand tool, Quick Mask mode, or a combination of both to create an alpha channel for each image.

4. Save the image, noting in the file name that the graphic has an alpha channel.

   The table on the following page lists the files you need to create alpha channels for, the recommended tool to cut the alpha channel with, and any special procedures required.

File Name	Suggested Tool	Special Procedure
1 - Pipe.tif	Magic Wand	Save as a 16x9 image
2 - Guitar.tif	Magic Wand	Crop so guitar is as large as possible, save as a 4x3 image
3 - Palette.tif	Magic Wand	Save as a 4x3 Image
4 - Tulips.tif	Magic Wand and Quick Mask	Save as a 4x3 image
5 - Mardi Gras Mask.tif	Magic Wand and Quick Mask	Save as a 4x3 image
6 - Astronaut.tif	Magic Wand and Quick Mask	Remove the background sky, save as a 4x3 image
7 - Bear.tif	Quick Mask	Remove all but the bear and the foreground tree, save as a 4x3 image
8 - Fisheye Cow.tif	Quick Mask	Leave only the cow head in the alpha, save as a 4x3 image
9 - AvidProNet.png	Magic Wand	Convert to RGB, do not resize, do not include the white portion in the alpha

Module 4

Editing with Alpha Channels

You are ready to import alpha channels into Avid Xpress DV. Because Avid Xpress DV imports an image with an alpha channel as a nested effect, you can edit the background and foreground video layers separately.

Objectives

After you complete this module, you will be able to:

- Import images with alpha channels into Avid Xpress DV

- Modify the contents of an imported matte effect

Importing Graphics with Alpha Channels

Graphics that contain alpha channels are imported in the same manner as graphics without alpha channels. However, it is important that the Import options are properly configured for the alpha channel.

1. Select the bin where you want to store the imported files.

2. Choose File > Import.

   The import dialog box appears.

   Windows

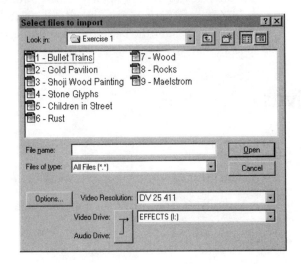

Macintosh

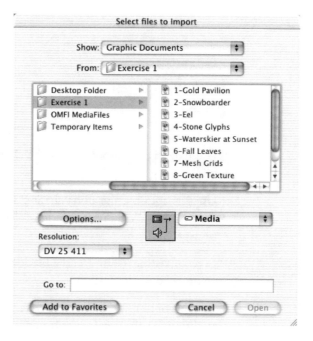

3. Navigate to the folder where the import elements are stored.

4. Select the file(s) to import.

   (Windows) To select multiple files: use the Control or Shift keys to select multiple files at once. The control key allows you to select discontiguous files while the shift key allows you to select contiguous files.

   (Macintosh) To select multiple files: use the Shift key to select multiple files at once.

5. Choose the Media Drive and Resolution.

6. Click the Options button to open the Import Settings dialog box.

Configuring the Alpha Channel Option

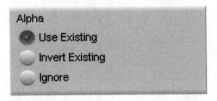

- **Use Existing** — Imports the alpha channel as it is saved in the file.

  Use this option if the alpha channel was configured using the Avid Xpress DV-native definition (black for opaque, white for transparent).

- **Invert Existing** — Inverts the black and white areas in an alpha channel before importing it.

  Use this option if the alpha channel was configured using the traditional definition (white for opaque, black for transparent).

- **Ignore** — If this option is selected, the system disregards the alpha channel and imports only the RGB portion of the image.

1. Select the appropriate Alpha option.

2. Refer to Module 2 for information on the other import options.

3. When you are satisfied with the Import Settings, click OK to return to the Import dialog.

4. Click OK to begin the import process.

Using Imported Matte Keys

When you import a graphic file, sequential graphic file, or video clip with an alpha, a Matte Key effect with source appears in the selected bin.

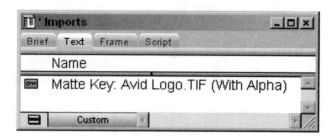

Once imported, edit the graphic as you would a clip. When you view the graphic in the timeline, the clips on lower tracks show through the transparent areas of the alpha channel.

If the matte key is inverted (the lower tracks are showing through the shape of the foreground instead of the background), you need to import it again, using the correct alpha import option. Improperly created matte keys cannot be inverted inside Avid Xpress DV.

Modifying an Imported Matte Key's Contents

You can see and modify the foreground and alpha matte elements by stepping into the imported matte key.

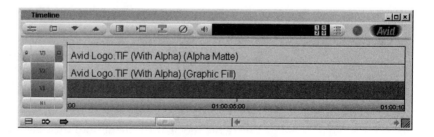

The foreground is located on V2 inside the nest and can be replaced with another still or video clip.

The matte element is located on V3 inside the nest. This track is locked and you cannot directly modify it. If you need to modify the matte element separately, you must first "unlock" the alpha matte element.

"Unlocking" the Matte Element

You cannot directly unlock the alpha channel by using the Unlock Track command from the Clip menu. Before you can modify it, you must copy it out of the nest.

1. Park the position indicator on the imported matte effect and make sure this track is active.

2. Step into the Matte Key effect and park in the middle of it.

3. Activate V3 and deactivate V1 and V2.

4. Click the Mark Clip button to mark all of V3.

5. Press the C key on the keyboard to copy the alpha channel into the clipboard.

6. Choose Tools > Clipboard Monitor to display the alpha channel in a pop-up monitor.

7. Step out of the effect.

8. Park on the first frame of the effect.

9. Click on the Remove Effect button to remove the Matte Key effect.

   When you remove the Matte Key effect from an Imported Matte Key the footage on V2 remains. You can replace this footage with any other clip media, if desired.

10. Add a new video track and patch the source to the new track.

11. Overwrite the matte element onto the track just above the Matte Key effect.

12. From the Effect Palette, apply a Matte Key effect to the matte element.

The timeline should now look similar to the following illustration.

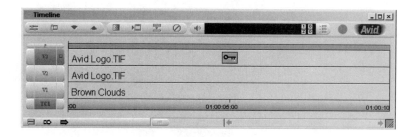

Animating the Matte Element

To animate the matte, you must step into the newly applied Matte Key and apply an appropriate effect.

1. Step into the new Matte Key effect.

2. Apply a Resize to the matte element.

3. Enter Effect mode.

4. Open the Background Color parameter and set the Luminance to 255.

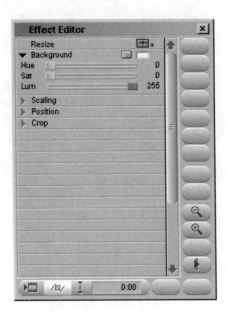

This step ensures that white will be visible around the edges of the matte element when you animate it.

5. Use the Resize parameters to animate the matte element.

Review Questions

1. What is the difference between the traditional matte key designation and Avid Xpress DV's native designation? *(See "Configuring the Alpha Channel Option" on page 4-4.)*

2. What happens if a graphic with an alpha channel is imported using the incorrect alpha import setting? *(See "Using Imported Matte Keys" on page 4-5.)*

3. What must you do to correct the above situation?*(See "Using Imported Matte Keys" on page 4-5.)*

4. How do you replace the graphic fill with a video clip? *(See "Modifying an Imported Matte Key's Contents" on page 4-5.)*

5. Why is it necessary to set the Background parameter to white when animating a matte element? *(See "Animating the Matte Element" on page 4-7.)*

Exercise 4

Using Alpha Channels in Effects

In this exercise, you will experiment with different ways of working with the alpha channel graphics you created in the previous exercise.

Importing Matte Keys

1. Import all of the graphics with alpha channels you created in the previous exercise.

   - Import the first eight files with the Import option, Aspect Ratio, Pixel Aspect set to *601, non-square.*

   - Import the final file with the Import option, Aspect Ratio, Pixel Aspect set to *Maintain, square.*

     The final graphic is grabbed created for a web site. It is the wrong size and would be distorted if 601, non-square was selected.

2. Load the imported graphics into the Source monitor and confirm that they all imported correctly.

   If they didn't, see if you can figure out what went wrong.

   Common mistakes include:

   - not creating all alpha channels with the same designation (white on black or black on white)

   - failing to properly size and crop the image

   - forgetting to save the alpha channel altogether

3. If necessary, correct the graphics in Photoshop and reimport them.

Using an Alpha Channel as a Custom Wipe

Though Avid Xpress DV includes many common wipe patterns, you can use third party programs to create customized wipe patterns to use in your video. In this exercise, you are going to use the alpha channel from the Fisheye Cow graphic to create a custom bovine-shaped iris wipe between two clips.

You are going to construct this effect using checkerboarded edits. Although you usually use this editing style with audio, you can also use it to speed up the design of certain types of vertical effects.

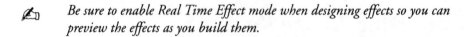 *Be sure to enable Real Time Effect mode when designing effects so you can preview the effects as you build them.*

Defining the Shape

1. Create a new sequence.

2. Open the **Fall in Wisconsin** bin.

3. Load **Shoreline Pan** into the Source monitor.

4. Mark a three second duration and splice it into the sequence.

5. Choose Clip > New Video Track.

6. Patch to V2 of the sequence.

7. Load **Farm Pan** into the Source monitor.

8. Mark a two second duration from the end of the clip and splice it onto V2 of the sequence.

Your Timeline should look like the following illustration:

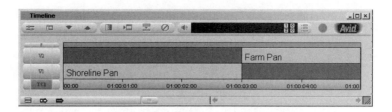

9. Choose Clip > New Video Track.

10. Patch to V3 of the sequence.

11. Load the Fisheye Cow matte key you imported earlier into the
    Source monitor and mark a two second duration.

12. Control+Alt+click (Windows) or Command+Option+click
    (Macintosh) on the end of the Wheatfield Pan clip to park on the last
    frame of the segment in the timeline.

13. Mark an OUT.

14. Overwrite the Fisheye Cow graphic onto V3.

    Your Timeline should look like the following illustration:

Extracting the Alpha Channel

This effect uses only the alpha channel of the Fisheye Cow graphic. The existing image of the cow can be discarded.

1. Park on the Fisheye Cow matte and click the Step In button to step into the effect.

2. Select V3 and deselect V1 and V2.

3. Click on the Mark Clip button to mark the entire alpha channel.

4. Press the C key on the keyboard to copy the alpha channel into the clipboard.

5. Choose Tools > Clipboard Monitor to display the alpha channel in a pop-up monitor.

6. Click the Step Out button to step out of the effect.

7. Click the Mark Clip button to select the Fisheye Cow graphic.

8. Overwrite the alpha channel over the Fisheye Cow graphic.

9. Select the Key effect category in the Effect Palette and apply a Matte Key effect to the alpha channel on V3.

   Now you need to edit in the source video for the effect. Because you built the effect in a checkerboard style, all you have to do is trim back the head of the **Flowers Pan** clip until it lies underneath the matte completely.

10. Enter Trim mode and select the head of the **Flowers Pan** clip. Make sure to select both sides of the edit for trimming.

11. Trim the head of the shot back two seconds.

Your Timeline should look like the following:

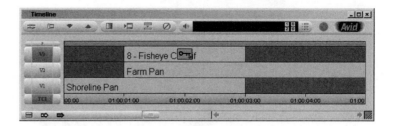

Animating the Wipe Shape

The final step required is to animate the size of the alpha channel so that the cow head shape wipes from the first shot to the second. In order to resize just the alpha channel, we need to step into the Matte key effect and apply a Resize directly to the matte element.

1. Step into the new Matte Key effect.

2. Apply a Resize to the matte element.

3. Enter Effect mode.

4. Open the Background Color parameter and set the Luminance to 255.

5. Open the Scaling parameter pane and set the X and Y scaling to 0.

6. Select the last keyframe and increase the X and Y parameters until the black portion of the matte fills the screen.

7. Play the resize effect and check the animation.

   The shape should grow to fill the entire screen.

8. Step out of the Matte key effect.

9. Play the sequence to see the final effect.

Rendering the Effect

This particular effect will not render correctly if Real Time Effects are enabled. However, if you disable Real Time Effects, this effect will render correctly.

1. Click the Real Time Effects button in the upper right corner of the Timeline to disable Real Time Effects.

   • When Real Time Effects are enabled, the button glows green.

   • When Real Time Effects are disabled, the button is dark blue.

2. Park on the matte key effect and press the Render Effect button to render the effect.

3. Click the Real Time Effects button again to re-enable Real Time Effects.

   Real Time Effects should be enabled for the remainder of the exercise.

Creating a Graphic Wipe

You are working on a music video. The video producer would like to use a graphic of an Epiphone guitar to wipe between two shots in the video. This effect can be easily accomplished by compositing two different effects:

• A graphic wipe to wipe between the two shots

• A graphic of the guitar that travels diagonally across the screen

   The graphic of the guitar should be keyframed so it tracks the wipe.

Creating the Graphic Wipe

Avid Xpress DV includes a basic diagonal wipe, but the angle of the guitar graphic we want to use is different than the angle of the wipe. As the angle is not adjustable, we can use Photoshop to create a matte element at the proper angle and then use Avid Xpress DV to animate the matte. The first thing we should do is create the diagonal wipe shape. We will do this by creating an alpha channel that diagonally divides the screen along the center line of the guitar.

Creating the Diagonal Wipe Shape

1. Launch Adobe Photoshop.

2. Open the graphic you created of the Guitar in Exercise 3.

3. Click on the Create New Channel button at the bottom of the Channels palette to create a second alpha channel.

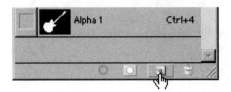

The new alpha channel is automatically selected and displayed.

4. Click on the eyeball next to the original alpha channel to also view it.

With both alpha channels displayed, you can use the shape of the guitar matte to help line up the position and angle of the diagonal wipe shape.

5. Press on the Rectangle tool and select the Line tool from the pop-up tool list.

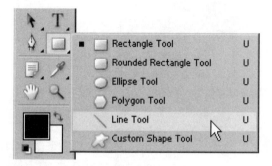

You can also press Shift+U repeatedly to toggle through the shape tools until you reach the Line tool.

As the new alpha channel is solid black, by default, we should use white for the color of the matte edge.

6. Press D to reset the foreground and background colors to black and white, respectively, and then press X to switch the two colors.

7. Position the cursor on the strap knob on the bottom of the guitar and press the mouse button down.

8. Drag the mouse diagonally up the center of the guitar and off the edge of the image to create a line.

   Now you need to finish the diagonal line so it also goes off the bottom left edge of the image.

9. Position the mouse on the middle of the line you just drew, press the mouse button, and drag the mouse off the bottom left edge of the image, using the existing line as a your guide.

Your image should look like the following illustration:

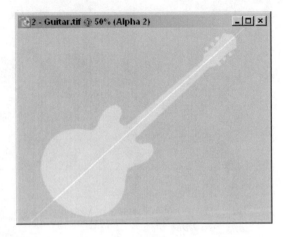

Finalizing the Diagonal Wipe Shape

1. Drag the original alpha channel to the Channels palette trash icon to delete it as it is no longer necessary.

2. Press the W key to select the Magic Wand tool.

3. Click on the upper left portion of the image to select it.

4. Choose Select > Modify > Expand, select 1 pixel, and click OK.

5. Press Alt+Backspace (Windows) or Option+Delete (Macintosh) to fill the selected area with white.

 Alt+Backspace (Windows) or Option+Delete (Macintosh) fills the selected area with the foreground color. As white is the current foreground color, the selected area is filled with white.

6. Choose File > Save As... and name the new file **Guitar Wipe matte.tif.**

7. Switch to Avid Xpress DV and import the new file into your project.

    Don't forget to set the options to invert the alpha channel on import.

Laying out the Sequence

As we did in the previous effect, we will checkerboard the two video clips. This time, however, we'll edit the clips in with the overlap instead of using Trim later to add the overlap.

Editing in the video clips:

1. Create a new sequence name it **Guitar Wipe**.

2. Add two new video tracks (for a total of four).

3. Open the **Carbon Leaf** bin and load the **Bassist** clip into a pop-up monitor.

4. Mark a two second duration from the beginning of the clip and edit it onto V1 of the sequence.

5. Back up one second in the timeline and mark an IN.

6. Load the **Singer** clip into a pop-up monitor, mark a two second duration from the end of the clip.

7. Edit the clip onto V2.

Editing in the imported graphics:

The two graphics will be edited in on V3 and V4. The wipe shape should be the same duration as the overlap on V1 and V2 while the guitar graphic must begin earlier and end later. This is because the guitar graphic is wider than the wipe edge. The wider the wiping graphic, the earlier it has to start before the wipe and the later it has to end after the wipe. We will use a five frame overlap on each side for this effect.

1. Park in the middle of the overlap of the two clips, hold the Alt key (Windows) or Option key (Macintosh) down and press Mark Clip.

   The Alt or Option key instructs Avid Xpress DV to mark the shortest duration across all clips. As we are in the middle of the overlap, the head of the **Singer** clip is used for the IN and the tail of the **Bassist** clip is used for the OUT.

2. Edit the **Guitar Wipe matte.tif** graphic onto V3.

3. Load the matte key you created from the **2-Guitar.tif** file into the Source monitor and patch to V4 in the sequence.

4. Park on the edit at the head of of the **Singer** clip, back up five frames, and mark an IN.

Remember that you can hold the Control key (Windows) or Command key (Macintosh) down and click near an edit to snap to the head of an edit.

5. Park on the edit at the tail of the the **Bassist** clip, move forward four frames and mark an OUT.

   You only need to move forward four frames because, by parking on the head of an edit, your OUT point is already one frame beyond the end of the clip. Avid Xpress DV edit points always include the frame you are parked on.

6. Edit the matte key you created from the **2-Guitar.tif** file onto V4.

   Your sequence should look like the following illustration:

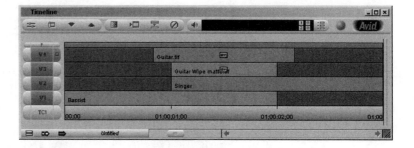

Setting up the Wipe

We only need the matte of the wipe shape on V3. We can extract the alpha channel as we did in the previous effect.

1. Select V3 and deselect all other tracks.

2. Park on the Guitar wipe matte and click the Step In button to step into the effect.

3. Select V3 and deselect V1 and V2.

4. Click on the Mark Clip button to mark the entire alpha channel.

5. Press the C key on the keyboard to copy the alpha channel into the clipboard.

6. Choose Tools > Clipboard Monitor to display the alpha channel in a pop-up monitor.

7. Click the Step Out button to step out of the effect.

8. Click the Mark Clip button to select the Guitar wipe matte graphic.

9. Overwrite the alpha channel over the Guitar wipe matte graphic.

10. Select the Key effect category in the Effect Palette and apply a Matte Key effect to the alpha channel on V3.

Animating the Wipe

The wipe needs to travel diagonally across the frame. We can do this by animating the matte element.

1. Step into the Matte Key effect on V3.

2. Apply a Resize effect to the matte element and enter Effect mode.

3. Press the Zoom out button to reveal the area around the video frame.

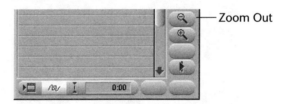

4. Open the Scaling pane and set the Horizontal and Vertical Scaling parameters to 210.

   This ensures that the matte is large enough to be always visible when you animate it.

5. Select the first keyframe and drag the object up and left until the lower right edge is just off the edge of the frame as shown in the following illustration.

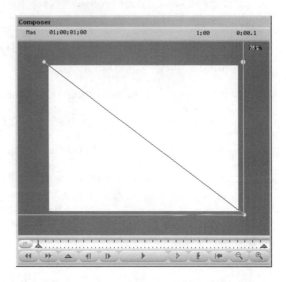

6. Select the last keyframe and drag the object down and right until the upper left edge is just off the edge of the frame as shown in the following illustration.

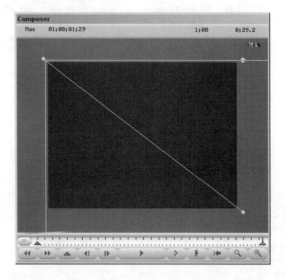

7. Step out of the nest.

Animating the Guitar Graphic

Now you need to animate the guitar graphic so that it tracks the wipe animation.

1. Select the guitar matte on V2.

2. Open the Scaling parameter pane and set the X and Y scaling to 125.

    This makes the guitar a little larger so it is nearly as wide diagonally as the video frame. You may need to use a different Scaling value, depending upon how you cropped the graphic.

3. Select the first keyframe and drag the guitar graphic until it is just off the top left corner of the frame.

4. Select the last keyframe and drag the guitar graphic until it is just off the bottom right corner of the frame.

5. Scrub through the effect to see how closely the guitar tracks the wipe.

    If you were lucky in your positioning, the wipe edge will be hidden by the guitar body and neck. More likely though, the wipe edge is either a little ahead or a little behind the guitar.

Fine-Tuning the Guitar Graphic Animation

Getting the guitar graphic timing right is a matter of trial and error. Both the starting and ending positions may need adjusting.

1. Examine the first half of the effect to assess problems with the starting position.

    *   If the guitar is behind the wipe, the starting position needs to be moved closer to the edge of the frame.

    *   If the guitar is ahead of the wipe, the starting position needs to be moved away from the edge of the frame.

2. Park on the first keyframe and adjust the starting position until it appears to be properly set.

3. Examine the second half of the effect to assess problems with the ending position.

   - If the guitar is behind the wipe, the ending position needs to be moved away from the edge of the frame.

   - If the wipe is guitar is ahead of the wipe, the ending position needs to be moved closer to the edge of the frame.

4. Park on the last keyframe and adjust the ending position until it appears to be properly set.

5. Scrub through the effect and confirm that the guitar correctly tracks the wipe.

6. If necessary, readjust the starting or ending positions until the guitar animation is correct.

7. Render the effect on V4 and play the finished effect.

Creating a Hold-Out Matte

You are working on a spot for Bullfrog sunscreen products. You are almost finished with the spot, but the producer is unhappy with the final product shot. She doesn't think the product stands out enough against the background. She suggests that you try darkening the background of the video but leave the bottle and the foreground rocks unaffected.

To accomplish this effect, you will create what is often referred to as a *hold-out matte*. You will export a frame of the clip out to Photoshop and create the matte as an alpha channel. Then you will use that alpha channel to isolate the background of the video from the foreground, enabling you to apply a Color Effect to the background only.

Exporting from Avid Xpress DV

The first step is to export the video frame as a TIFF file.

1. Load the **Bottle Splash** clip from the **Bullfrog** bin into a pop-up monitor.

2. Place the Position Indicator at a point where you can see the edges of the bottle without the splash obscuring it.

3. Choose File > Export.

4. Click on the Options button to open the Export options dialog.

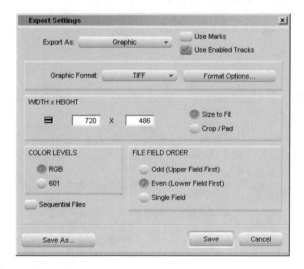

5. Set the Export File Type to Graphic and choose TIFF from the Graphic Format pop-up menu.

6. Set the size to 720 x 480 (NTSC) or 720 x 576 (PAL).

7. Click Save to store the Export Settings.

8. Name the file "Bullfrog Bottle.tif" and save it.

Creating the Mask in Adobe Photoshop

You'll apply the techniques you learned earlier to create an alpha channel for your image. Here are the steps:

1. Launch Adobe Photoshop.

2. Open **Bullfrog Bottle.tif.**

3. Create the alpha channel for the file using the techniques covered in Module 3.

   The alpha channel should isolate the bottle and foreground rocks from the rest of the image.

4. Select File > Save As, name the file "Bullfrog Bottle alpha.tif" and save it as a TIFF file.

Building the Sequence

1. Return to Avid Xpress DV.

2. Load the original **Bottle Splash** clip into a pop-up monitor.

3. Mark an IN at the beginning of the clip and an OUT at the end.

4. Splice the shot onto V1 of a new sequence.

5. Import the graphic you created into your import bin.

   Be sure to set the alpha channel import option correctly.

6. Mark the duration of the sequence and create a new video track.

7. Load the imported Bullfrog graphic into a pop-up monitor and patch it to V2 of the sequence.

8. Overwrite in the matte key onto V2.

Using the Holdout Matte

If you were to monitor V2 and play the sequence, you'll notice that the bottle and foreground rocks are a still image over a moving background. You must replace the graphic fill with the **Bottle Splash** clip.

1. Park in the middle of the sequence and confirm that V2 is active.

2. Click the Step In button to step into the effect.

   Inside the effect are three tracks. V2 is the Graphic fill and V3 is the alpha channel.

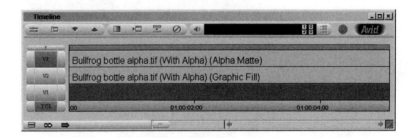

3. Deselect V1 and V3 and park the position indicator on the middle of the sequence.

4. Click Mark Clip to mark the duration of the graphic fill.

5. Reload the **Bottle Splash** clip into a pop-up monitor.

6. Patch to V2 of the sequence and Overwrite to replace the graphic fill with the Bottle Splash clip.

7. Click the Step Out button.

   The water now splashes in front of the bottle. All that is left is to use a Color Effect to darken the background.

Applying a Color Effect to the Lower Track

1. Open the Effect Palette and select the Image category.

2. Apply a Color Effect to the **Bottle Splash** clip on V1.

3. Enter Effect mode.

4. Select the Color Effect on V1.

5. Open the Luma Range parameter and lower the Gamma to darken the video.

   You might also want to manipulate other parameters, such as Chroma Saturation, until you have a look you are pleased with.

6. Move the Position Indicator to various points in the clip to preview the effect.

7. Leave Effect mode.

8. Confirm that you are monitoring V2 and play the sequence to view the finished effect.

Module 5

Using Photoshop Layers

Adobe Photoshop allows you work with separate graphic *layers*. You can think of each layer as an acetate sheet, each containing different graphic elements such as shapes, text, or textures, and stacked one on top of the others. The bottom layer is called the *background* layer. It remains below the others; any layer you add above it will obstruct it partially, depending on its placement, contents, and transparency.

Objectives

After you complete this module, you will be able to:

- Describe what a layer is in Adobe Photoshop

- List several benefits to working with layers

- Create layers from an alpha channel

- Edit a text layer

- Work with images that have multiple layers

- Save layered Photoshop files

Working with Layers

The main benefit to working with layers is that you can edit each layer independently, meaning that you can draw, copy, paste, and move elements as well as apply blending techniques, add text, and so on. If all the elements were in one layer, it would be difficult to separate one from the other and make adjustments. Another benefit to working with layers is that you can create separate text layers, and edit the text using text tools rather than paint tools. This makes it much easier to try out different ideas.

Finally, if you work with layers, you can take advantage of Adobe Photoshop's layer effects such as glows, shadows, or bevels. We will cover these techniques in the next module.

Layers and Alpha Channels

In Module 2, we created an alpha channel from a full-frame opaque image. This full-frame image is called the Background layer in Photoshop. The alpha channel defines the opacity and transparency of the Background layer.

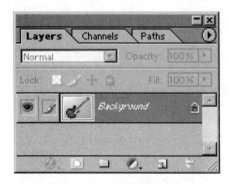

 To display the Layers palette, choose Window > Show Layers.

Once you begin working with layers, the alpha channel becomes less important. Each layer contains an invisible alpha channel that defines opacity and transparency of the layer. When working with layers, alpha channels are not required and can be deleted.

Converting an Image with an Alpha Channel Into a Layer

Before you can manipulate an object using layers, you must convert the image and its alpha channel into a layer.

1. Open the image file in Adobe Photoshop.

2. Select Window > Show Channels.

   The Channels palette appears.

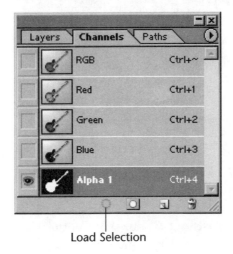

Load Selection

3. Click on the alpha channel to select it.

4. Load the alpha channel as a selection by clicking on the Load Selection button at the bottom of the Channels palette.

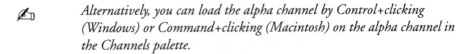   *Alternatively, you can load the alpha channel by Control+clicking (Windows) or Command+clicking (Macintosh) on the alpha channel in the Channels palette.*

   If the alpha channel is black on white (saved using Avid Xpress DV's native method with black representing opaque and white representing transparent), you need to invert the selection so the foreground is selected.

5. If the selection needs to be inverted, Press Control+Shift+I (Windows) or Command+Shift+I (Macintosh) to invert the selection.

   If the alpha channel is created white on black, you can skip this step.

6. Click the Layers tab.

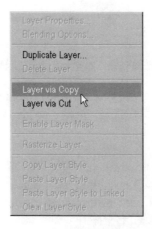

If you cannot locate the Layers palette, open it by choosing Window > Show Layers.

7. Right-click (Windows) or Control+click (Macintosh) on the Background layer and select Layer via Copy.

A new layer is created that contains the area defined by the alpha channel. You can now manipulate this object independently. The background layer and the alpha channel are no longer required and can be deleted, if desired.

8. (Optional) Drag the alpha channel to the Trash button in the lower right hand corner of the Channels palette.

9. (Optional) Drag the Background layer to the Trash button in the lower right hand corner of the Layers palette.

Working with Type Layers

Adobe Photoshop's Type tool allows you to add type to an image.

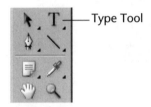
Type Tool

1. Open the image to which you want to add text.

2. Select the Type tool by clicking on it in the Tool Palette or by pressing T on the keyboard.

   The Type tool options are displayed below the menu bar.

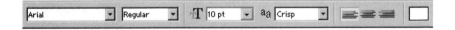

3. If desired, adjust the type characteristics (font, point size, and so on) using the Type tool options bar.

   Photoshop allows you to create either point type or paragraph type. Point type is useful to add a few words while paragraph type allows you to enter paragraphs of type.

4. Click the cursor at the location you wish to add text to create point type.

If you would rather create paragraph type, click and drag the cursor to create a text box.

When click on the image, a text layer is automatically created and placed above the active layer. A "T" appears next to the layer name, indicating the layer is a Type layer.

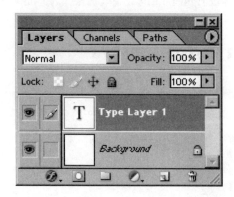

5. Enter the desired text.

   If necessary, select the text and change the type characteristics, using the options bar.

   To kern the text (adjust the horizontal spacing between two letters), hold the Alt key (Windows) or Option key (Macintosh) down and press the right or left arrow.

6. Press the Enter key on the numeric keypad or click the OK button in the options bar commit your changes.

   Optionally, you can choose any other tool in the Tool palette or click on another layer in the Layers palette.

Working with Type Layers

Editing Text

Once a Type layer has been created, the text can be easily modified or changed.

1. Select the Type tool.

2. Click on the text in the image window to activate the type layer and set the insertion point.

3. Select and adjust the text as desired.

4. Press the Enter key on the numeric keypad or click the OK button in the options bar commit your changes.

Changing the Text Color

The color of the text can be changed for the entire type layer or for an individual character or group of characters.

1. Select the Type tool.

2. Select the desired text using one of the following procedures:

   • Click on the desired type layer to select the entire layer.

   • Click on the text in the image window to activate the type layer. Then select the desired character(s).

   Click on the Text Color box in the options bar.

Text Color

The Photoshop Color Picker opens.

3. Choose the desired color from the Color Picker and click OK.

Rasterizing Type Layers

Some commands and tools, including the painting tools, are not available for type layers. The type layer must be rasterized and converted into a normal layer before these tools can be used.

1. Select the desired type layer in the Layers palette.

2. Right click (Windows) or Control+click (Macintosh) on the desired layer and choose Rasterize Layer from the pop-up menu.

   The type layer is converted to a normal layer.

Working with Multiple Layers

The following sections describe several useful techniques for working with multiple layers.

Layered Files and Avid Xpress DV

Avid XpressDV 3 (or higher) can import Photoshop files with layers as either a flattened composite image or a sequence with each layer on a separate video track. However, not all layer settings and adjustments are preserved.

These restrictions will be discussed in detail later in this module and in Module 6. However, in the following section we will call out the limitations and restrictions as they apply to the layer manipulations discussed.

Selecting a Layer

To edit a layer, you must first select it to make it active.

■ To select a layer, click the layer name in the Layers palette.

Showing or Hiding Layers

Layers can be displayed or hidden. The eye icon in the Layers palette indicates whether a layer is visible or hidden.

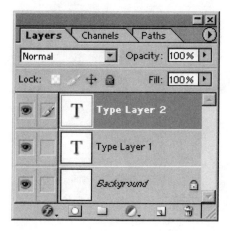

■ To hide a layer, click the eye icon next to a layer.

■ To show a hidden layer, click in the empty space in eye column next to the layer.

Hidden layers only stay hidden when the file is imported as a flattened image. Hidden layers will be visible when the file is imported as a sequence of layers.

Rearranging Layers

The layer order determines whether a layer appears or in front of other layers. You can easily rearrange the layers by dragging.

 You cannot move the Background layer or place a layer below the Background layer.

1. In the Layers palette, select the layer you want to move.

2. Drag the layer up or down.

As the layer moves past other layers, a solid line will appear between the layers indicating the new layer position.

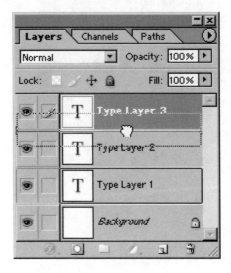

3. Release the mouse when the layer is in the layer is in the desired position to reorder the layer.

Duplicating a Layer

Duplicating a layer makes it easy to store two versions of a layer in one file.

To duplicate a layer:

1. Right click (Windows) or Control+click (Macintosh) on the layer and select Duplicate Layer.

The Duplicate Layer dialog appears.

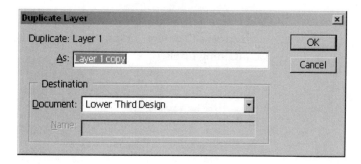

2. Enter a name for the duplicate layer and click OK.

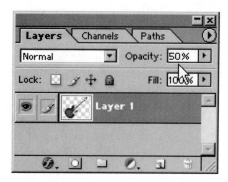   *Optionally, you can duplicate a layer by dragging the layer to the New Layer button at the bottom of the Layers palette.*

Setting Layer Opacity

Each layer has its own defined opacity which is adjusted using the Opacity field at the top of the Layers palette.

1. Select the layer you wish to adjust.

2. Click in the opacity field and enter the desired opacity.

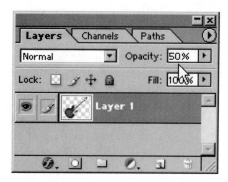

Layer opacity is only interpreted correctly if the file is imported as a sequence of layers.

Locking Transparency

The Transparency lock allows you to protect the boundaries of objects in a layer and therefore confine painting and editing to areas of the layer containing pixels.

 Transparency locking is not available for type layers. The type layer must first be rasterized.

To Lock a Layer's Transparency

1. Select the desired layer.

2. Click the transparency lock checkbox (the left most lock icon).

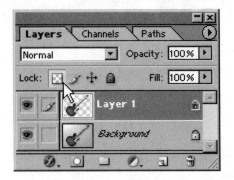

Blending Modes

You can modify a layer's *blending mode* to control how the layer's pixels are mixed with lower layers and create different lighting or color effects.

1. Select the layer whose blending mode you wish to adjust.

2. Click on the blending mode pop-up menu in the Layer palette to display the available blending modes.

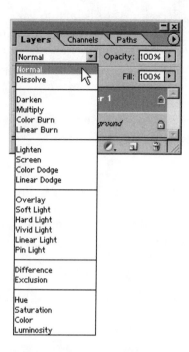

3. Choose one of the blending modes from the list.

You can also apply blending modes to the painting tools from the Paintbrush Options window. For example, if you set the mode to Hue, you can replace the colors in a layer with a single color, while preserving all luminance information.

Blending modes are not preserved when the file is imported as a sequence of layers. To preserve a layer's blending mode, merge the layer with a lower layer. Layer merging is discussed later in this module.

Clipping Groups

For certain effects it may be helpful to have a single object boundary, or mask, for multiple layers. This allows you to restrict the paint or effect to the edges of an object, but leaves the additional paint or effect independently editable. You do this by grouping layers together in a *clipping group*.

When creating a clipping group, the lowest layer, or *base* layer, acts as the mask for the entire group. All layers in the group must be adjacent to one another.

To create a clipping group

1. If necessary, rearrange the layers so the base layer is below the other layers you want to group.

2. Select the base layer.

3. Activate the Link switch for every other layer you want to include in the group.

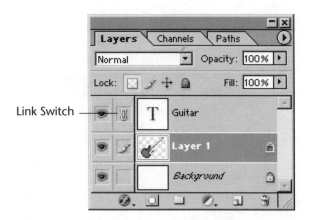

Link Switch

4. Press Control+G (Windows) or Command+G (Macintosh) to group the layers.

   The layers are grouped together. Notice that the grouped layers are slightly indented in the layers palette and the line between the two is now dotted.

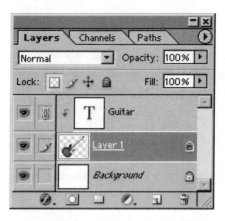

Any pixels on layers grouped within a master layer will only display where pixels exist in the master layer. For example, if the illustration below, if the Text layer is grouped with the image of the guitar, the text is only visible where the guitar exists.

Layers not grouped

Layers grouped together

You cannot view a grouped layer independently of its master. You can, however, ungroup layers at any time by selecting one of the grouped layers and typing Control+Shift+G (Windows) or Command+Shift+G (Macintosh).

Clipping groups are not preserved when the file is imported as a sequence of layers. To preserve a clipping group, merge the grouped layers with the base layer. Layer merging is discussed later in the next section.

Merging Layers

Sometimes it is useful or necessary to combine two or more layers into a single layer. The merge commands allow to you combine different groups of layers. Two merge commands are available, Merge Down and Merge Visible.

To Merge Two Layers:

1. If necessary, rearrange the two layers so they are adjacent to one another.

2. Select the higher of the two layers.

3. From the Layers palette fast menu, choose Merge Down or press Control+E (Windows) or Command+E (Macintosh) to combine the two layers into one.

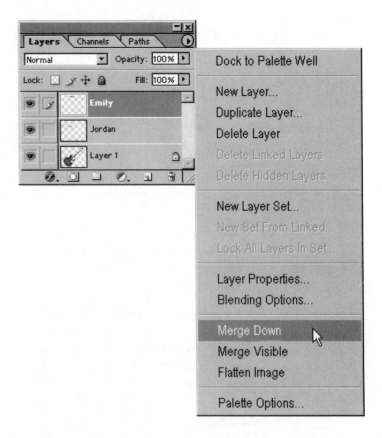

▲ Text layers must be rasterized before they can be merged together.

To Merge Multiple Layers:

1. Hide any layers you do not wish to merge by clicking on the eye icon next to the layer.

2. From the Layers palette fast menu, choose Merge Visible or press Control+Shift+E (Windows) or Command+Shift+E (Macintosh) to combine all the visible layers into one.

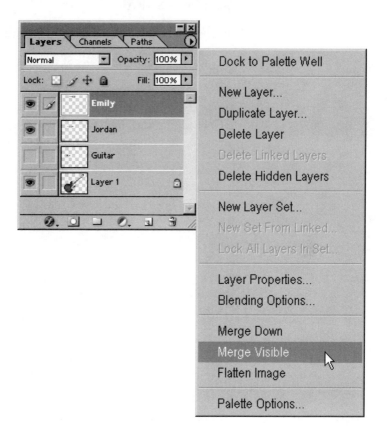

Saving Files with Layers

If you wish to preserve the individual layers, the file must be saved using Photoshop's native format. If you choose another file format, Photoshop will save the composite of all layers. For maximum flexibility, we recommend saving files with layers in the Photoshop format.

Saving as a Photoshop file

1. Choose File > Save As.

2. If necessary, navigate to the folder you wish to save the files in.

3. Select Photoshop from the list of formats in the Format pop-up menu.

    Do not select Photoshop EPS, Photoshop DCS, or Photoshop PDF. These are variants of the Photoshop file format designed for print and are not supported for import into Avid Xpress DV.

    Notice that the Save Option *Layers* is checked at the bottom of the Save dialog. Photoshop automatically assumes you want to include the layers in the saved file.

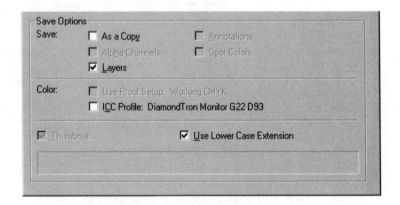

4. Click Save.

    Photoshop saves the file to the selected destination.

Importing Layered Files into Avid Xpress DV

 The Photoshop file must contain more than one layer for the layered file import dialog to appear. Files with only one layer will be imported as a standard graphic file.

When a layered Photoshop file is imported into Xpress DV an import option dialog appears.

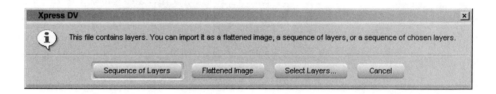

- Choose Sequence of Layers to import each layer separately.

  Each layer will be imported as a still graphic with alpha and a sequence will be created containing the layers in the order they appeared in the Photoshop file. The individual files are assigned the name of the layer and the sequence is assigned the name of the file.

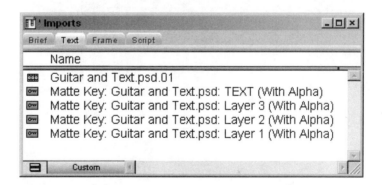

- Choose Flattened Image to import the file as a single graphic with alpha.

  All layers will be merged together and an alpha channel representing the composite of all layers will be created.

▲ Note: If the file does not contain a Background layer and an alpha channel, some elements will have a white halo around them. This is due to the fact that the fill and matte generated by Photoshop for the flattened image are encoded as a premultiplied alpha. Individual layers, on the other hand, are encoded as a straight alpha. Avid Xpress DV does not support premultiplied alpha channels for import.

If you need to work with a composite of a multilayered file, you should create an alpha channel and choke the alpha as described in Module 3.

- Choose Select Layers... to import only some of the layers in the file.

If this option is selected, a dialog box appears listing the layers contained within the file.

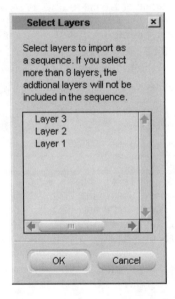

- Click on a layer to select it for import.

- Click on a selected layer to deselect it.

Up to 8 layers can be selected and imported.

Photoshop Layer Options and Avid Xpress DV

As mentioned earlier in this module, not all layer options and types are supported for import. The following table lists all the Photoshop layer options and indicates whether they are supported for import. Unless otherwise noted, the following table only applies to files imported as a sequence of layers.

Layer Option	Supported	Notes
Blending Mode	Normal only	To preserve the blending mode, merge the layer into another layer that does not use a special blending mode.
Opacity	Yes	The imported layer's Level is set to the opacity specified in Photoshop.
Layer Group	Partial	Layer grouping is ignored. All layers, including grouped layers, are imported as individual layers. To preserve a clipping group, merge the grouped layers into the base layer.
Layer Set	Partial	All layers within a set are imported as individual layers. Note: Layer sets are not covered in this course.
Layer/Set Mask	No	Layer and set masks are ignored. To preserve a layer mask, apply it to the layer. To preserve a set layer, merge the set into an empty layer. To preserve a special layer's mask, apply the layer mask. Note: Layer mask application and usage are not covered in this course.
Layer Style	No	Layer styles are ignored. To preserve a layer style, you must convert the style into layers. Layer styles are covered in detail in Module 6

Special Layer Types and Avid Xpress DV

Most of Photoshop's layer types are supported for import in Avid Xpress DV. The following table lists the special Photoshop layer types and indicates whether they are supported for import. With the exception of the Type layer, none of the special layer types are covered in this course. This table is provided for future reference.

Layer Type	Supported	Notes
Type Layer	Yes	
Solid Layer	Yes	Solid layers are imported as a graphic with a full screen opaque alpha channel.
Gradient Layer	Yes	Gradient transparency is preserved.
Pattern Layer	Yes	
Adjustment Layer	No	

Review Questions

1. What is the main benefit to working with layers in Adobe Photoshop? *(See "Working with Layers" on page 5-2.)*

2. How do you convert a graphic with an alpha channel into a layer? *(See "Converting an Image with an Alpha Channel Into a Layer" on page 5-3.)*

3. Why would you want to rasterize a text layer? *(See "Rasterizing Type Layers" on page 5-8.)*

4. What is a clipping group? *(See "Clipping Groups" on page 5-14.)*

5. What are the two different ways Avid Xpress DV can import a layered Photoshop file and how are they different? *(See "Importing Layered Files into Avid Xpress DV" on page 5-19.)*

Exercise 5

Working with Layers

Creating a Safe Title/Action Grid Overlay

As you remember from Module 1, it is important to ensure that all relevant information is kept within safe title or safe action. In this first section, you'll create a Safe Title/Action grid overlay that can be used to help ensure your graphics will be visible on a standard television screen.

1. Create a new file with the correct frame size for NTSC or PAL. Set the contents of the new file to White.

2. Choose Select > All or press Control+A (Windows) or Command+A (Macintosh).

3. Choose Edit > Free Transform or press Control+T (Windows) or Command+T (Macintosh).

   The options bar displays the transform options.

Scale Options

4. In the Scale options, enter 90 percent for Width and Height.

   If you click the chain icon between the two options, they are locked together and update simultaneously.

5. Press the Enter key on the numeric keyboard to perform the scale.

You may need to press the Enter key twice, once you confirm the field value of 90 and again to perform the scale.

6. Choose Select > Modify > Border.

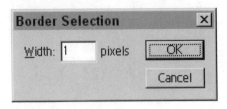

7. Enter a width of 1 pixel and click OK.

8. In the Layers palette, click the Add Layer button.

9. Click on the Foreground Color button in the tool bar and choose a color for the Safe Action line.

10. Choose Edit > Fill.

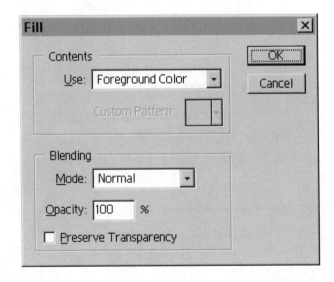

11. Choose Foreground from the Contents pop-up menu. and click OK.

The Safe Action boundary is now displayed with a line of the color you selected. Next you will create a line for Safe Title.

Creating the Safe Title Line

1. In the Layers palette, select the Background layer.

2. Repeat steps 2 through 11 from the previous two pages, this time using 80 percent as the scale amount.

   If desired, use a different color for the Safe Title line.

3. Delete the background layer by dragging it to the Layer window's trash.

4. Merge the two layers together by choosing Layer > Merge Visible or pressing Control+Shift+E (Windows) or Command+Shift+E (Macintosh).

5. Double-click on the layer name in the Layer palette to select the layer's name.

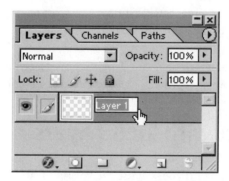

6. Name the layer "Safe Title/Action Grid."

7. Save this file and name it "Safe Title/Action Overlay (XxY)."

   Substitute (XxY) with the dimensions of the title you created the overlay for. For example, (640x480).

Using the Safe Title/Action Overlay

You can overlay this layer on top of other images to see if the contents fits within the desired boundaries. This requires pasting the Safe Action/ Safe Title layer onto a new layer in the destination file.

▲ **The overlay and the image file must have the same dimensions.**

1. Open both the overlay and the image files.

2. In the overlay file, press Control+A (Windows) or Command+A (Macintosh) to select the entire overlay.

3. Press Control+C (Windows) or Command+C (Macintosh) to copy the overlay.

4. Click on the image file to activate it.

5. Press Control+V (Windows) or Command+V (Macintosh) to paste the overlay into the new file.

 Though the safe action/title layer is useful when working in Photoshop, you should delete it prior to importing the file into Avid Xpress DV.

Experimenting with Text Layers

In this section you will use the layering features of Photoshop to modify the graphics you originally created and create new graphics.

Creating a Lower Third with Text and Graphics

Your need to create a lower third title for a program on painting that includes the host's name, Emily Brogan, with a graphic of a paint palette.

1. Open the graphic of the paint palette that you created in Exercise 3 and, using the steps in Module 5, create a layer for the palette.

2. Delete the original alpha channel and the Background layer as they are no longer required.

3. Insert the Safe Title/Action Overlay you created earlier into this file to use as a guide.

4. Use the Type Tool to create a text layer with the words "Emily Brogan."

   The text should rest at the lower edge of the Safe Title area. Depending upon the font you use, the point size should be between 60 and 90 points. You are free to use any font and color.

   You can use the Move Tool in the toolbox (also accessed with the V key on the keyboard).

5. Select the layer containing the palette graphic.

6. Press Control+T (Windows) or Command+T (Macintosh) to enter Free Transform mode.

7. Use the handles to resize the palette so that it is slightly taller than the "E" in the word *Emily.*

   Hold the Shift key while resizing the palette to constrain the proportions of the graphic. If you make a mistake, hit the Escape key to cancel the transformation.

   You can move the image while transforming by dragging the image.

8. Press the Enter key on the keyboard when you are satisfied with the size and position of the palette to complete the transform.

9. Adjust the position of the palette so that it is at the lower-left corner of Safe Title; then, adjust the position of the text so that it is to the immediate right of the palette.

10. Delete the Safe Title/Safe Action guide layer as it is no longer needed.

Finalizing the Graphic

Currently, the image of the palette and the text are on two separate layers. If you want to manipulate them as a single lower third element, the two layers need to be merged together into one. In this instance, we want the two parts of the lower third to be stored separately and as a merged element. This maximizes the flexibility within Avid Xpress DV.

1. From the Layers palette, Right-click (Windows) or Control+click (Macintosh) on the layer containing the paint palette graphic and select Layer Properties.

2. Name the layer "Palette" and click OK.

3. Right-click (Windows) or Control+click (Macintosh) the Palette layer and select Duplicate Layer.

4. Right-click (Windows) or Control+click (Macintosh) the Emily Brogan text layer and select Duplicate Layer.

5. Rearrange the two duplicate layers so they are adjacent and above the two original layers.

6. Select the higher duplicated layer and press Control+E (Windows) or Command+E (Macintosh) to merge the two layers together.

7. Right-click (Windows) or Control+click (Macintosh) the merged layer and select Layer Properties.

8. Name the merged layer "Palette and Name" and click OK.

9. Select File > Save As or press Control+Shift+S (Windows) or Command+Shift+S (Macintosh) and give the file an appropriate name.

Filling Text with a Texture

By using clipping groups you can fill text with a graphic texture.

1. Select File > New to display the New File dialog.

2. Enter the appropriate size for NTSC or PAL.

3. Choose Transparent from the Contents options.

4. Use the Type Tool to create a text layer.

   Use any word or words you choose. Adjust the size so that the text is as large as possible to fit within Safe Title.

5. Open one of the graphic texture files you saved in Exercise 1.

6. Press Control+A (Windows) or Command+A (Macintosh) to select the entire file and Control+C (Windows) or Command+C (Macintosh) to copy the texture.

7. Close the graphic texture file.

8. Paste the texture into file containing the text you typed.

   It will be pasted into a new layer.

9. If necessary, rearrange the layers so that the graphic texture layer is the topmost layer.

10. Link the texture and the text layer together by selecting one of the two layers and clicking on the Link switch on the other.

11. Press Control+G (Windows) or Command+G (Macintosh) to group the two layers together.

    The texture is now only visible where the text appears.

12. If desired, unlink the two layers and use the Move tool (V on the keyboard) to reposition the texture within the text.

Finalizing the Graphic

Avid Xpress DV does not maintain clipping groups in Photoshop files. The grouped layers must be merged together.

1. Select the texture layer.

2. Press Control+Shift+E (Windows) or Command+Shift+E (Macintosh) to merge the two layers together.

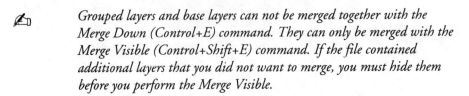

Grouped layers and base layers can not be merged together with the Merge Down (Control+E) command. They can only be merged with the Merge Visible (Control+Shift+E) command. If the file contained additional layers that you did not want to merge, you must hide them before you perform the Merge Visible.

The file now contains only one layer. As mentioned earlier, the file must have two layers or it will not be imported as a layered file into Avid Xpress DV.

3. Select the Text tool and create a new Text layer.

4. Type "Dummy" to indicate this is a dummy layer and not part of the actual design.

   The extra layer must contain something or it will not be seen as a layer by Avid Xpress DV. If you prefer to use a regular layer, use the Paint tool to add a stroke or dot to the layer.

5. Save the file.

Using Blending Modes

Blending modes allow you to control how layers composite with one another. We will use blending modes to "burn" text into an image. In this particular exercise, the producer wants you to burn John Lennon's name onto an Epiphone guitar.

1. Open the Guitar image you created in the Exercise 3.

2. Create a layer from the alpha channel and delete the Background layer and the alpha channel.

3. Select the background layer and fill it with White.

4. Use the Type Tool to create a text layer that reads "John Lennon."

   The text should be on two lines. Adjust the leading, if necessary, so the two lines are tightly spaced. Set the text color to yellow.

5. Use Transform mode (Control+T (Windows) or Command+T (Macintosh)) to resize and rotate the text until it fits on an unadorned portion of the guitar body.

6. Select the text layer and change the Blending mode to Overlay.

   The text is burned into the guitar. Notice how it picks up the different shades and textures of the wood.

7. Use the Move tool to drag the text around the body.

   Notice how the luminance changes in the guitar affect how the text is displayed. For example, as you drag the text over the guitar strings, notice that the text turns bright yellow and that it almost disappears when on top of the dark areas.

8. Change the Blending mode to Soft Light.

9. Drag the text around the guitar body and notice how the text blends in differently.

10. Experiment for a few minutes with other Blending modes and text colors.

    Select the text tool and the layer to change the text color.

Finalizing the Graphic

Avid Xpress DV ignores layer blending modes. In order to maintain the effect, the text layer must be merged with the guitar layer.

1. Select the text layer.

2. Press Control+E (Windows) or Command+E (Macintosh) to merge the two layers together.

The file now contains only one layer. As mentioned earlier, the file must have two layers or it will not be imported as a layered file into Avid Xpress DV.

3. Select the Text tool and create a new Text layer.

4. Type "Dummy" to indicate this is a dummy layer and not part of the actual design.

    The extra layer must contain something or it will not be seen by Avid Xpress DV. If you prefer to use a regular layer, use the Paint tool to add a stroke or dot to the layer.

5. Choose File > Save As... and save the file with a different name.

Importing the Images into Avid Xpress DV

The files you created are ready for import into Avid Xpress DV. Two of the files you created, the textured text and the text burned into the guitar, have a dummy layer which will not be used in Avid Xpress DV. If desired, these layers can be ignored during import.

1. Launch Avid Xpress DV and select the Import bin.

2. Choose File > Import.

3. Select the graphics you created in this exercise and select Open to begin the import process.

The layered file options dialog appears.

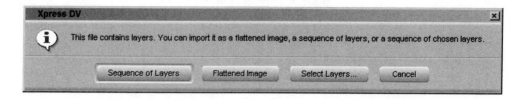

4. Choose Select Layers to display the select layers dialog box.

   Depending upon the order you selected the files, the dialog will either display the three layers in the lower third graphic, or the two layers in one of the other two graphics.

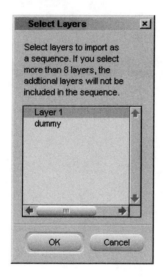

5. Select the appropriate layers and click OK to continue the import process.

6. Continue importing the remaining graphics.

If desired, you can import all of the graphics as a sequence of layers. This option requires less user interaction, but will import the dummy layers. The dummy layers should be deleted after they are imported.

7. Create a sequence, edit some video into V1, and edit the graphics you imported onto the higher tracks.

8. If desired, experiment with keyframing with some of the graphics to animate them.

9. Try compositing the graphics you just created with the original versions.

   For example, try layering the original guitar graphic with the new text-enhanced graphic. Use the Level parameter to fade the text in and out.

Module 6

Creating Layer Styles and Actions

Photoshop allows styles, or effects, to be applied to individual layers, making it very easy to create effects such as bevels, shadows, and glows. Though these are designed to create effects for a Photoshop composite, you can also use them to create elements that can be composited in Avid Xpress DV. Additionally, you can use Photoshop actions to automate the creation of these and other effects.

Objectives

After you complete this module, you will be able to:

- Create a bevel on text or graphics

- Create a drop shadow for an image

- Create a glow for an image

- Create a video bevel

- Use Photoshop actions to automate multi-step Photoshop procedures

Creating Beveled Text and Graphics

Adding a bevel to text or graphics adds the perception of depth and can make flat text more dynamic and interesting.

1. Create a new file using the following using the following criteria:

    • Use the proper frame size for NTSC or PAL.

    • Set the file contents to Transparent.

2. Type the desired text using the Type Tool.

    Optionally, you can convert a graphic to a layer using the procedures in Module 5. Be sure to delete the Background layer after you have converted the graphic to a layer.

3. Choose Bevel and Emboss from the Layer Style fast-menu at the bottom of the Layers palette.

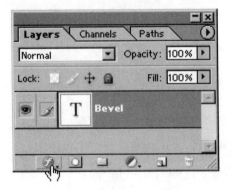

The Layer Style dialog opens.

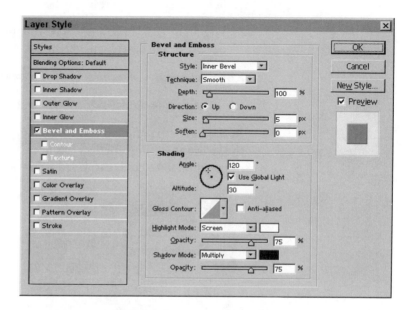

The style can be adjusted using the following parameters:

- **Style** — determines the type of bevel or emboss. Inner Bevel is the most appropriate choice for text and graphics.

- **Technique** — sets the type of bevel applied.

  - Smooth creates a softened beveled edge.

  - Chisel Hard creates a hard, knife-like edge and creates a nice three dimensional effect when applied to type.

- **Depth** — increases the prominence of the bevel. Increasing depth results in whiter highlights and blacker shadows.

- **Direction** — determines whether the bevel is projected outward or inward.

- **Size and Soften** — Controls how wide the bevel is and how hard or soft bevel edge is.

The Size and Soften parameters, when selected, can be adjusted with the up and down arrows on the keyboard.

- **Angle** and **Altitude** — allow you to adjust the position of the light source used to create the beveled effect.

- **Highlight** and **Shadow** — allow you to adjust set the color and opacity of the bevel highlight and shadow.

4. Experiment with the settings until you are pleased with the look.

5. Click OK to close the dialog and apply the style.

   In the Layers palette, an Effect icon appears on the right side of the layer indicating an effect has been applied and a description of the applied effect is displayed below the layer.

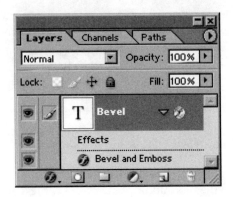

 You can collapse the effect description by clicking on the triangle to the left of the Effect icon in the layer.

Finalizing the Graphic

Since Avid Xpress DV does not support Layer Effects, you need to convert the layer and effect into a basic layer. This is most easily accomplished by merging the layer and effect with an empty layer.

1. Click on the Create Layer button to create an empty layer.

2. Press Control+Shift+E (Windows) or Command+Shift+E (Macintosh) to merge the two layers together.

   The now contains only one layer. As mentioned earlier, the file must have two layers or it will not be imported as a layered file into Avid Xpress DV.

3. Select the Text tool and create a new Text layer.

4. Type "Dummy" to indicate this is a dummy layer and not part of the actual design.

5. Save the file as a Photoshop file.

Creating a Drop Shadow

Soft-edged drop shadows are very popular for text and graphics. Adding a drop shadow to a graphic element can help it "pop out" from the background. The following steps illustrate how to add a drop shadow to text. You can also use these steps to add a drop shadow to a graphic layer.

1. Create a new file using the following using the following criteria:

   • Use the proper frame size for NTSC or PAL.

   • Set the file contents to Transparent.

2. Type the desired text or convert the graphic to a layer.

3. Choose Drop Shadow from the Layer Style fast menu at the bottom of the Layers palette.

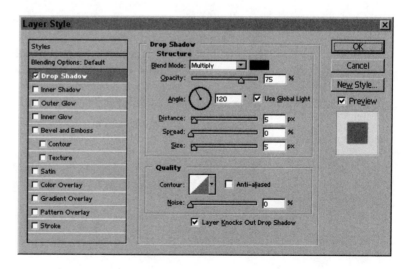

The style can be adjusted using the following parameters:

- **Color** — located to the right of the blend mode, this allows you to set the color of the drop shadow.

- **Opacity** — controls how transparent or opaque the shadow is.

- **Angle** and **Distance**— sets the location of the shadow.

The location of the shadow can also be set by dragging the shadow in the image when the Layer Style dialog is displayed.

- **Size** — determines the amount of blur in the drop shadow.

- **Spread** — can be used to restore fine details, such as letter descenders, that may be have disappeared in the blur.

The Size and Spread parameters, when selected, can be adjusted with the up and down arrows on the keyboard.

4. Experiment with the settings until you are pleased with the look.

5. Click OK to close the dialog and apply the style.

Finalizing the Graphic

As with the bevel effect, the effect must be converted to layers so it will be imported into Avid Xpress DV. In this instance, we will create a layer for a combined text and shadow and separate layers for the text and the shadow. This maximizes flexibility within Avid Xpress DV.

1. Right click (Windows) or Control+click (Macintosh) the layer's effect icon and choose Create Layer.

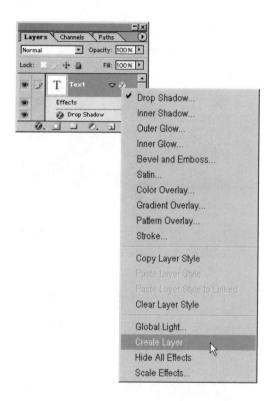

▲ This is not the same as clicking the Create Layer button in the Layers palette. This function actually separates the shadow from the image.

Photoshop will display a warning that not all aspects of an effect can reproduced with layers.

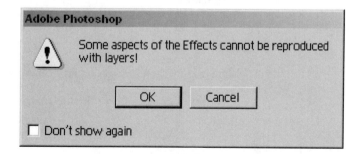

The warning is not relevant to the effect we are creating.

2. Click OK to close the warning.

   The Drop Shadow effect is converted to a layer.

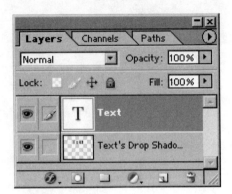

   If you select the shadow layer in the Layers palette, you will notice that the opacity of the layer is the opacity you specified in the layer effect (75% by default). This opacity will be carried over to Avid Xpress DV.

3. Right-click (Windows) or Control+click (Macintosh) the Text layer and select Duplicate layer.

4. Right-click (Windows) or Control+click (Macintosh) the Drop Shadow layer and select Duplicate layer.

5. Rearrange the two duplicate layers so they are adjacent and above the two original layers.

6. Select the higher duplicated layer and press Control+E (Windows) or Command+E (Macintosh) to merge the two layers together.

7. Right-click (Windows) or Control+click (Macintosh) the merged layer and select Layer Properties.

8. Name the merged layer "Text and Shadow" and click OK.

9. Select File > Save and give the file an appropriate name.

Creating a Glow

Glows around text and graphic elements are another commonly requested effect. A popular variation is to use black as the glow color for text. The following steps describe how to add a glow to text. You can also use these steps to add a glow to a graphic layer.

1. Create a new file using the following using the following criteria:

    *   Use the proper frame size for NTSC or PAL.

    *   Set the file contents to White or Background Color.

    When creating a glow, it is easier to see and modify it if the background is black (or a dark color) instead of transparent. (If you are planning on creating the black glow effect, leave the background white.)

2. Choose Edit > Fill and fill the background with black.

    Optionally, you can choose a dark color for the foreground or background color and fill with that instead.

3. Use the Type Tool to create a text layer for this effect.

4. Chose Outer Glow from the Layer Style fast menu at the bottom of the Layers palette.

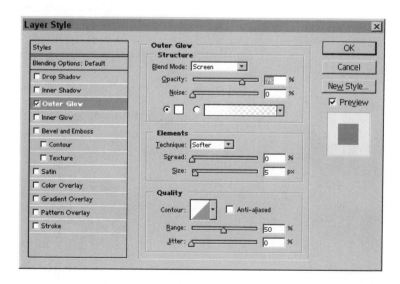

Use the following parameters to adjust the glow effect:

- **Opacity** — sets the opacity of the glow.

- **Noise** — adds grain to the glow.

- **Color** — click in the color box to set the glow color. Optionally, select a gradient pattern from the gradient pop-up list to create a multi-color glow.

- **Technique** — sets the type of glow applied.

  - Softer creates a blurry glow that does not precisely follow the contours of the object

  - Precise creates a glow that closely follows the contours of the object. It is particularly useful when adding a glow to text or complex logos.

- **Size** — sets the size of the glow.

- **Spread** — can be used to restore fine details, such as letter descenders, that may have disappeared in the glow. Large values of spread create a solid halo around the object.

The Size and Spread parameters, when selected, can be adjusted with the up and down arrows on the keyboard.

- **Contour** — allows you to control the opacity transition of the glow or create multiple rings in the glow.

- **Range** — controls how the contour is applied to the glow.

5. Experiment with the settings until you are pleased with the look.

6. Click OK to close the dialog and apply the style.

Finalizing the Graphic

As with the drop shadow, the effect must be converted to layers so it will be imported into Avid Xpress DV. As before, we will create a layer for the combined text and glow and separate layers for the text and the glow.

1. Right click (Windows) or Control+click (Macintosh) the layer's effect icon and choose Create Layer.

   The Glow effect is converted to a layer.

2. Right-click (Windows) or Control+click (Macintosh) the Text layer and select Duplicate layer.

3. Right-click (Windows) or Control+click (Macintosh) the Drop Shadow layer and select Duplicate layer.

4. Rearrange the two duplicate layers so they are adjacent and above the two original layers.

5. Select the higher duplicated layer and press Control+E (Windows) or Command+E (Macintosh) to merge the two layers together.

6. Right-click (Windows) or Control+click (Macintosh) the merged layer and select Layer Properties.

7. Name the merged layer "Text and Glow" and click OK.

8. Delete the Background layer as it is no longer needed.

9. Select File > Save and give the file an appropriate name.

Creating a Video Bevel

Though similar to the first effect we created in this exercise, this effect creates an element that bevels the video in Avid Xpress DV. This effect is often used to create logo bugs in the corner of the screen but you can also use it to create a whole host of effects in a video composite. For example, you can use it to bevel a company logo onto a moving background.

Because Photoshop assumes that compositing will occur in Photoshop, there are quite a few steps involved in creating this effect element. Follow the instructions carefully as one skipped step can cause the entire effect to fall apart.

Creating the Bevel Effect

1. Create a new file using the following using the following criteria:

   - Use the proper frame size for NTSC or PAL.

   - Set the file contents to Transparent.

2. Use the Type Tool to create the text layer to be used in this effect.

   The text color is not relevant as we will be exporting only the bevel itself. Optionally, you can use any graphic object or EPS file instead of text. (We will discuss importing EPS files in the next module.)

3. If using a Type layer, right click (Windows) or Control+click (Macintosh) on the layer and choose Rasterize Layer from the pop-up menu to convert the layer to a normal layer.

   This option is required to perform some of the later steps in this procedure.

4. Choose Bevel and Emboss from the Layer Style fast menu at the bottom of the Layers palette.

5. In the dialog box, choose Inner Bevel, and adjust the other parameters as desired.

See "Creating Beveled Text and Graphics" on page 6-2. for more information on configuring the Bevel style.

Creating the Video Bevel Elements

Because we are going to create a video-only bevel, we need to break the effect apart to isolate the bevel parts from the graphic or text element.

1. Right click (Windows) or Control+click (Macintosh) the layer's effect icon and choose Create Layer.

This separates the effect into two layers — one for the bevel highlights and one for the bevel shadows. Notice that this effect uses a clipping group.

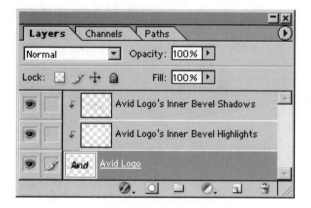

The bevel shadow and highlight elements are ready, but we need to modify the graphic element to make it a partially transparent gray. This helps the video bevel be *read* by the viewer.(If desired you can leave in full color, but it is usually preferable to convert the logo to a gray shape.)

2. Select the object layer and click on the Lock Transparent Pixels switch to activate it.

   This switch preserves the shape of the object.

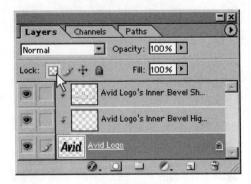

3. Choose Edit > Fill... to display the Fill dialog.

   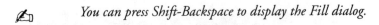 *You can press Shift-Backspace to display the Fill dialog.*

4. Set the Fill to 50% Gray and click OK.

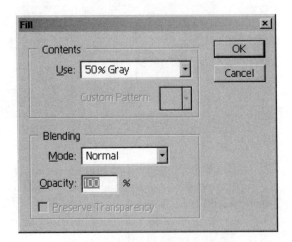

Now you need to reduce the opacity of the graphic element. Photoshop provides two different opacity adjustments for a layer, Opacity and Fill. Though these operate similarly for regular layers, they function differently when adjusting a group's base layer.

- **Opacity** — reduces the opacity of all layers in the group, including the base layer.

- **Fill** — reduces the opacity of the base layer only. The grouped layers are unaffected.

In this case, we only want to reduce the opacity of the base layer. If we reduced the opacity of all layers, the bevel elements would no longer be visible.

5. Set the Fill of the graphic layer to 30%.

   This is a suggested value and works well for most objects. You may want to experiment with other opacity values.

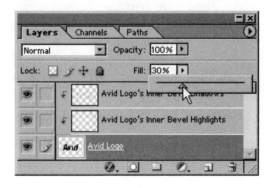

Finalizing the Graphic

As this effect is most easily used as a single element in Avid Xpress DV, we need to merge the layers together and create a dummy layer.

1. Press Control+Shift+E (Windows) or Command+Shift+E (Macintosh) to merge the three layers together.

2. Select the Text tool and create a new Text layer.

3. Type "Dummy" to indicate this is a dummy layer and not part of the actual design.

4. Save the file as a Photoshop file.

Using Photoshop Actions

You can automate most repetitive tasks in Photoshop by creating an *action*. Actions are macros that repeat a series of steps at the click of a button. Because several steps are involved in the effects we created earlier in this module, it makes sense to automate them with an action.

Photoshop allows you to organize your actions into *sets* in the Actions palette. Before we start creating our first action, we should create a Video Actions set.

1. Choose Window > Show Actions to open the Actions palette.

2. Press the Create New Set button at the bottom of the Actions palette and name the new set **Video Actions**.

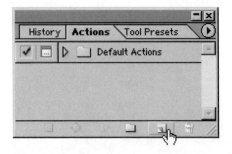

Recording a Photoshop Action

Now we are ready to record an action. We will create a new action and then execute the various steps in order.

1. Create a new file or open an existing file with an object you want to modify.

2. If necessary, create a text element or convert an alpha channel into a layer.

3. If you are working with a text or previously named layer, rename the layer Layer 1 by clicking the right arrow to the right of the Layers palette and choosing Layer Options from the menu.

4. In the dialog box that appears, type "Layer 1" into the name field.

   This step is necessary as Photoshop refers to layers by name in an action. If you record an action with a specific layer name, the action will fail when you play it back if it does not find a layer of the specified name. "Layer 1" is the default name given to the first created layer in Photoshop.

   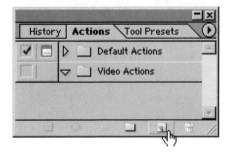 *If the file only contains one layer (and no Background layer) and all files the action will be run on contain only one layer, the above step can be recorded as the first step of the action.*

5. Click the Create New Action button.

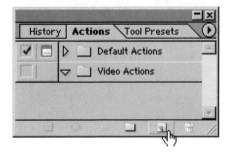

6. Name the action with the name of the effect you are going to record (For example: Bevel, Drop Shadow, Glow, Video Bevel, and so on.).

7. Select the Video Actions set from the Set pop-up menu.

   If desired, assign a function key to the action.

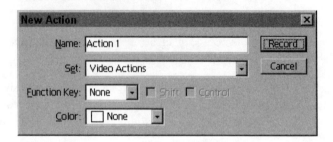

8. Click Record.

9. Perform all of the steps for the effect you want to record. Refer to the steps earlier in this module for the desired effect.

   As you perform each step, it is recorded in the action.

 Do not record the Save or Save As step.

10. After you have recorded all the steps of the action, click the Stop Recording button in the Actions palette.

The action is now saved.

Playing an Action

After you have recorded an action, you can play it back.

1. Open the title or graphic for which you want to create a drop shadow or glow.

2. If necessary, create a layer from the alpha channel.

3. If necessary, rename the text or graphic layer to "Layer 1."

4. In the Actions palette, select the desired action.

5. Click the Play button.

Photoshop performs the action on the open file.

If you assigned a function key to the action, you need only open the file and click the desired function key.

Saving Actions

Actions are saved with the Photoshop settings on the system where they were created. It is a good idea to save your actions out to a file so you can keep a backup and use them on multiple systems.

1. Select the set you wish to save.

2. From the fast menu in the Actions palette, choose Save Actions.

   Actions are stored by default in the Presets\Photoshop Actions folder in the Photoshop program folder.

3. Name the set and click OK to save the set

   All action sets stored in the Presets\Photoshop Actions folder are listed at the bottom of the Actions palette fast menu. This makes it easy to quickly load and unload sets.

Review Questions

1. What is the most appropriate kind of bevel for text? *(See "Creating Beveled Text and Graphics" on page 6-2.)*

2. What happens when you choose Create Layer from the Layer menu while creating a drop shadow? *(See "Finalizing the Graphic" on page 6-6.)*

3. When creating a glow, why is it helpful to fill the background with black or a dark color? *(See "Creating a Glow" on page 6-9.)*

4. Give an example of when you might want to create a Photoshop action. *(See "Using Photoshop Actions" on page 6-16.)*

5. Why is it necessary to rename a layer to Layer 1 either before an action is run on it or as the first step of an action? *(See "Recording a Photoshop Action" on page 6-17.)*

Exercise 6

Working with Layer Styles

Layer Styles

In this exercise you will create all of the effects demonstrated in the previous module.

1. Using the steps in the previous module, create at least two of each of the following effects: beveled text, drop shadow, glow, and video bevel.

   You can either use the graphics you cut alpha channels for earlier or new files and text layers.

2. Record an action for either the drop shadow or the glow and play it back on another file.

3. Record an action for the video bevel and play it back on another file.

4. Import the images you created into Avid Xpress DV and edit them into a sequence. If desired, use keyframing to animate one or more of the images.

Module 7

Preparing EPS and PDF Files for Import

You may encounter graphic files that were saved in formats other than bitmap format. Because bitmap format is the only still graphic format that Avid Xpress DV accepts, you have to convert other files to bitmaps if you plan to import them. This module focuses on converting EPS and PDF vector-graphic files to bitmaps.

Objectives

After you complete this module, you will be able to:

- Convert files saved in EPS format to prepare them for import into Avid Xpress DV

- Convert files saved in PDF format to prepare them for import into Avid Xpress DV

Using EPS and PDF Files

EPS (Encapsulated PostScript) files are a special type of file that is created by graphic design programs such as Adobe Illustrator or Macromedia Freehand. These files do not contain bitmaps, or pictures of an image, but instead contain instructions describing how the image is actually drawn. The major advantage to this format is that, by containing only the instructions to draw an image, the image can be resized and drawn at any desired size. The same artwork designed for a stamp could be used for a poster or a billboard.

PDF (Portable Document Format) files are files created by Adobe Acrobat that store the information a printer needs to display and/or print a document. These files make it easy for a user to print and read a document even if they don't have the program or even the fonts used when creating the document.

Avid Xpress DV does not directly import EPS or PDF files. However, Adobe Photoshop provides a simple method to convert these files into a bitmapped graphic that Avid Xpress DV can import.

Font Issues With EPS Files

Type can be stored in an EPS file in two different ways.

- As a type block that references a specific font

  These EPS files can only be correctly converted if the font referenced in the graphic is installed on the system running Photoshop. If the font is not installed, the following message appears when you attempt to convert an EPS file.

If you select Continue, the EPS file is converted, but an installed font is substituted for the actual font. This is rarely the desired result.

- As the shapes of the individual letters

All programs that create EPS files have the ability to convert type to shapes, or outlines. When type is converted to outlines, the font is no longer required.

If you are given EPS files that reference fonts not installed on your system, you should inform the person who gave you the EPS file that they need to convert the type in the file to outlines and give you the converted file.

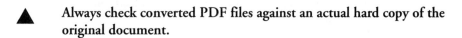 *Adobe Illustrator 10 and later can embed fonts into an EPS file. If the EPS file was created with Adobe Illustrator 10, the graphic artist can embed the fonts instead of converting the type to an outline.*

PDF File Issues

Type in PDF files is always stored as type referencing a specific font, but the required fonts can be embedded in the PDF file. Unfortunately, if the required font is not embedded, the font is substituted and no warning is given.

▲ **Always check converted PDF files against an actual hard copy of the original document.**

PDF files can also contain multiple pages. When a multi-page PDF file is converted, a dialog opens asking the editor to select the page to import.

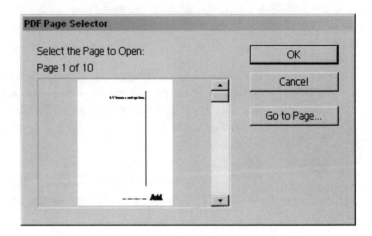

Converting EPS and PDF Files

To convert an EPS or PDF file, create a blank Photoshop file of the correct size and place the EPS or PDF file into that file. Though Photoshop can directly open EPS or PDF files, placing them into an existing file is more efficient as it allows you to size and place the image within the video frame.

1. Create a new file of the correct size for video.

2. Choose File > Place.

    The file dialog opens.

3. Choose the desired file from the list and click Place.

    The system places a preview of the image in the center of the frame. The preview is enclosed within a selection box with handles on the corners.

4. To move the image to another location, click within the preview and move the image to its new location.

5. To resize the image, grab one of the corner handles, hold the Shift key down, and drag the handle to resize the preview.

▲ **If you do not hold the Shift key down, or if you grab a side handle, you will distort the image.**

6. When you are satisfied with the size and position of the preview, press the Enter key on the numeric keypad to convert the image.

Photoshop converts the EPS or PDF file and places it on a new layer.

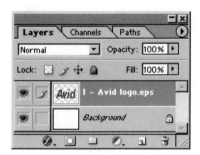

If you imported a PDF file, you may need to create an alpha channel for the image you are extracting.

7. (PDF only) Use the procedures described earlier in the book to create an alpha channel for the graphic.

Finalizing the Graphic

As the file likely contains only one layer, you will need to create a dummy layer or the file will not be imported as a layered file into Avid Xpress DV.

1. Select the Text tool and create a new Text layer.

2. Type "Dummy" to indicate this is a dummy layer and not part of the actual design.

3. Save the file as a Photoshop file.

Review Questions

1. What happens if a font required by an EPS file is not available when you attempt to place the file? *(See "Font Issues With EPS Files" on page 7-2.)*

2. How do you resize an image that you placed? *(See "Converting EPS and PDF Files" on page 7-4.)*

Exercise 7

Converting EPS and PDF Files

In this exercise, you will convert EPS files into TIFF files.

Converting The Files

Following the procedures in Module 7, convert the files in the **Exercise 7** folder.

The following table lists the files you need to convert and any special procedures required.

File Name	Special Procedure Required
1-Avid Logo.eps	Resize and place in lower right corner of frame, just inside safe action. Save graphic both as a color logo and as a video bevel.
2-Material Transit.eps	Add a glow around the image.
3-Momenteam.eps	Add a drop shadow to the logo.
4-DV Formats.pdf	Save only the logo at the bottom of page 1 of the PDF.

Module 8

Importing and Exporting Video

In this module, you'll learn how to export and import video with Avid Xpress DV. This allows you to take advantage of third party special effects packages such as Adobe After Effects, 3D animation packages, or others. You might also need to export the video for distribution on CD-ROM, DVD, or the web. Exporting for the web is covered in detail in Appendix A.

Objectives

After you complete this module, you will be able to:

- Describe the differences between square and nonsquare pixels

- Differentiate RGB Graphics levels from 601 video levels

- Convert graphics between the two mappings

- Describe the two most common import and export formats

- Import a movie file

- Export a sequence or clip

Additional Import and Export Options

Up until this point, importing and exporting have been relatively simple: crop and resize to a 4x3 or 16x9 aspect ratio, save, and import. However, we need to address three additional issues: nonsquare pixels, 601 levels, and alpha channel premultiplication. Both of these issues are relevant to all importing and exporting, but are particularly relevant to importing and exporting video and animation.

Square and Non-Square Pixels

When graphics and animations are created for use in Avid Xpress DV, they can be created using either square or non-square pixels. Avid Xpress DV uses non-square pixels internally.

Virtually all computer display cards use square pixels. Because the display uses square pixels, most graphic and animation programs also use square pixels. With square pixels, a 100 x 100 pixel box would be a perfect square.

But, digital video does not use square pixels. DV digital video standard uses a 720 pixel width for both NTSC and PAL. But, because NTSC and PAL have different numbers of scan lines (480 versus 576), digital video has pixels that are stretched vertically for NTSC and stretched horizontally for PAL.

The following graphic shows a close up of a circle drawn with square pixels and NTSC and PAL non-square pixels. Notice that the square pixel circle has the same number of pixels both horizontally and vertically, while the NTSC and PAL circles do not.

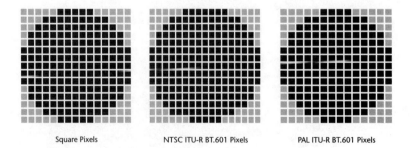

Square Pixels   NTSC ITU-R BT.601 Pixels   PAL ITU-R BT.601 Pixels

As mentioned previously, the native, non-square frame size for an Avid Xpress DV is 720 x 480 for NTSC and 720 x 576 for PAL. These frame sizes do not use square pixels.

Graphics and animations can be created with either square or non-square pixels. However, if the proper frame size is not used, the graphic or animation with be distorted when imported into the system. The following table lists the proper sizes for square and non-square pixel frames.

Format	Square Pixel 4x3	Square Pixel 16x9	Non-Square Pixel 4x3 and 16x9
NTSC	640 x 480	853 x 480	720 x 480
NTSC 601* (non-DV)	648 x 486	864 x 486	720 x 486
PAL	768 x 576	1024 x 576	720 x 576

NTSC 601 refers to the frame size of full-frame ITU-R BT.601 digital video. NTSC DV does not use the full frame. Instead, it omits off the top four lines and bottom two lines of the frame. Avid Media Composer, Symphony, and DS all use the full 601 frame size. PAL ITU-R BT.601 and PAL DV use the same frame size.

When you open an image that is saved with nonsquare pixels in a program such as Photoshop, which always displays using square pixels, the image appears stretched in NTSC or squeezed in PAL. This is normal, and is due to square pixels displaying a nonsquare pixel image.

Image Viewed in
Avid Xpress DV

Image Viewed in
Photoshop (NTSC)

Image Viewed in
Photoshop (PAL)

Nonsquare and Square Pixel Guidelines

The following guidelines should help you determine whether to use nonsquare or square pixels when importing and exporting.

Use nonsquare pixels when:

- Exporting video out of Avid Xpress DV.

  Because the DV frame is the native frame size for Avid Xpress DV, if you export using the proper nonsquare pixel size, there is no risk of artifacting due to a resize from nonsquare to square pixels.

- Creating animations and composites for import into Avid Xpress DV.

  You should always render animations and composites to the native frame size for the system you are importing into. We will discuss this in greater detail later in the module.

Use square pixels when:

- Preparing a still graphic for import.

  As illustrated in Module 1, sizing to a square pixel 4x3 or 16x9 aspect ratio is the simplest method and is appropriate for still graphics.

- Exporting a still graphic for use in print or on the web.

  Any image you plan to export for use in print or on the web should be at a square pixel size so it does not appear distorted when printed or displayed. You should also export only one field.

Video Levels for Imported Graphics and Animations

In Avid Xpress DV you can import and export animation, video, and still images using either RGB levels or ITR-R BT.601 levels. As an editor, you must understand the differences between the two choices and be able to communicate those differences to the people who are producing the graphics for your project.

When computer graphics are created, they are often created with absolute values for black and white. In 24-bit RGB (8 bits for each channel), black is assigned a value of 0 and white a value of 255. There is no allowance for values beyond either black or white.

However, the ITU-R BT.601 digital video standard does not treat black and white as absolutes—excursions above white and below black are allowed. To maintain full compatibility, Avid systems allow the creation of graphics using either computer graphics mapping (often referred to as RGB mapping) or ITU-R BT.601 mapping (referred to as 601 mapping).

RGB Mapping

RGB mapping assumes that video black (NTSC: 7.5 IRE, PAL: 0 mV) is assigned a value of 0 and video white (NTSC: 100 IRE, PAL: 700 mV) a value of 255. There is no allowance for excursions above these values. If an image is exported out of Avid Xpress DV using RGB mapping, any values below video black or above video white will be clipped. This results in the signal mapping as shown in the following illustration.

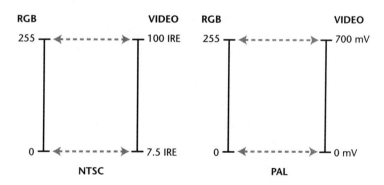

Most graphics and animation packages, including Adobe Photoshop and Adobe After Effects, assume RGB mapping. It is appropriate for graphics created for print and onscreen use, as black and white need to be absolute values. The concept of "whiter than white" or "blacker than black" does not come into play.

601 Mapping

The ITU-R BT.601 digital video standard allows for excursions beyond video black and video white. This ensures that some camera overexposure is maintained and to allow for sub-black values for luminance keying. The ITU-R BT.601 standard specifies that black is at 16 and white at 235. This allows for a reasonable amount of signal footroom and headroom and results in the signal mapping shown in the following illustration.

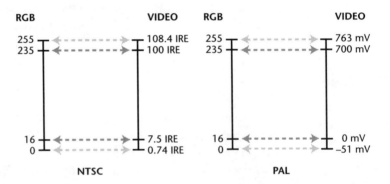

When a video signal is hard clipped at video black and video white, as it is with RGB Graphics mapping, undesirable "blooming" or flat regions often result. Additionally, slight "ringing" due to compression or analog filtering is often converted to blooming and therefore amplified. By using ITU-R BT.601 mapping, you can eliminate or dramatically reduce both of these problems.

Avid Xpress DV uses 601 mapping internally. If you need to maintain all of the video signal information when you export a clip, you should use 601 mapping. However, not all third-party programs natively understand this mapping. Extra care may need to be taken by the graphic artist, animator or compositor to make sure that the values for video black and video white are maintained and not allowed to extend into the headroom or footroom.

When importing graphics and animations, be sure to select the correct mapping. If the wrong mapping is chosen, the signal values will be incorrect. The following table describes what happens when the wrong mapping is chosen.

File Has:	Imported As:	Result
RGB values	601	Luma and Chroma is stretched—image appears to have greater contrast. Video black lowered to 0.74 IRE (–51 mV). Video white raised to 108.4 IRE (763 mV). Legal chroma may now be out of bounds.
601 values	RGB	Luma and Chroma is squeezed—image appears to have lower contrast. Video black raised to 14 IRE (50 mV). Video white lowered to 94 IRE (640 mV).

 You might want to establish a naming convention for graphics and animations created using 601 levels, perhaps adding "601" to the filename. (for example, Logo.601.tif)

601 and RGB Levels Guidelines

Avid Xpress DV allows you to export and import graphics and animations using either RGB or 601 levels. The following guidelines should help you determine when to use each mapping:

Use 601 levels when:

- Exporting a frame or frames that you plan to modify subtly and reimport.

  This method is appropriate when you need to fix a dropout or touch out negative grit. Using 601 levels maintains all of the captured signal. If you use RGB levels, the system clips all values below video black and above video white, which may introduce undesirable artifacts and cause the modified frame not to match back in perfectly.

- Using or creating video that requires superblack, such as a luma key element.

Use RGB levels when:

- Exporting a frame or frames that you plan to modify radically and reimport.

  One example is when you need to apply a stylize effect in Adobe Photoshop. Using RGB levels clips the signal at video black and video white, which is necessary in this case. If you use 601 levels, the effect you apply might cause the signal to extend beyond video black and white.

- Exporting a frame to be used in print or on the web.

Understanding Premultiplication

Premultiplication is a method by which the alpha channel is applied to the file's foreground, modifying the foreground. An easy way to understand premultiplication is to think of an alpha channel as a cookie cutter. Let's take a simple example where the file's foreground is a solid color and the alpha channel contains a logo. If the file was saved with a straight alpha, the foreground is left alone and only the alpha channel represents the logo's shape.

Foreground   Alpha Channel

When a file is premultiplied, the alpha channel is applied to the foreground. This is similar to using a cookie cutter to cut a shape out of a sheet of dough. The surrounding "dough" is removed and replaced with a specific color, usually black.

Foreground   Alpha Channel

Notice that the alpha channel is identical in both of the above images. Premultiplication does *not* affect the alpha, but instead affects the foreground.

Premultiplication is very easy to understand when the alpha channel is purely black and white with no intermediate grays. Now let's examine what happens when the alpha has gray, or partially transparent, areas. Imagine that our image is a blurred registration mark, as shown in the following illustration.

Foreground   Alpha Channel

The blurred edge is partially transparent and, when composited against another image, will be blended with the other image. Now let's look at how a compositing program renders the foreground and the alpha channel.

If the image is saved with a straight alpha, the shape of the registration mark is expanded so that the color of the object exists for every pixel of the object. This includes all of the partially transparent pixels, even those that are barely visible. The foreground looks like it was cut out by a fat version of the alpha. The illustration below shows what the foreground and alpha look like after rendering.

Foreground

Alpha Channel

Now let's look at the same image when rendered as a premultiplied alpha. In this case, when the alpha channel is applied to the foreground, the partially transparent areas are composited with a specific color, again usually black.

Foreground

Alpha Channel

Working with Straight and Premultiplied Images

Because the foreground is stored very differently for straight and premultiplied images, it is critical that the image be interpreted properly or it won't composite correctly. Let's take a look at how a compositing program interprets straight and premultiplied images.

Straight Alpha (Not Premultiplied)

The compositing of straight alphas is very straightforward. The alpha channel is applied like a cookie cutter to the foreground and the surrounding information is ignored. Because the color of the foreground exists for both opaque and partially transparent pixels, the color of the foreground is preserved.

Premultiplied Alpha

Remember that when an alpha channel is premultiplied the foreground is composited with black. If the foreground object was red, the partially transparent areas of the foreground were stored not as a pure red, but as a blending of red and black. Before the image can be composited against another image or a video clip, the black must be removed from the foreground. Compositing programs do this by applying an identical mathematical function to both the alpha channel and the foreground, in essence "unmultiplying" it. As this is a conform class and not a math class, we won't go into the math applied to the image.

Premultiplication Guideines

Avid editing systems do not know how to correctly interpret premultiplied alphas. Therefore, it is critical that animations be created using straight alphas.

If a premultiplied alpha is imported into Avid Xpress DV, artifacts will be visible. To illustrate these artifacts, we will take our image of the blurred registration mark and composite it against a solid color.

Because a straight alpha is used purely as a cookie cutter to extract the shape from the foreground, the foreground pixels are extracted exactly as they appeared in the foreground. Because transparent pixels in a premultiplied alpha image have been blended with black, this results in a black halo around the object. (If the image had be premultiplied with white, a white halo would be visible instead.)

Premultiplied interpreted as Straight   Premultiplied interpreted as Premultiplied

 Always create animations that will be imported into Avid editing systems using straight alphas.

Importing Video and Animation

Video and animation files are imported using the same method used when importing still graphics. Two different types of files can be imported.

- QuickTime or AVI movies

  Both QuickTime and AVI movies are single files containing all of the video or animation frames. These files can contain both video and audio information. QuickTime movies can also contain alpha channels.

- Sequential graphic files

  Sequential files are a series of files where each file represents a single frame. The file name includes a number that indicates the order of the frames. (For example, movie.000.tif, movie.001.tif, movie.003.tif, and so on.) Avid Xpress DV reads the numbering and uses it to order the files during import.

To Import Video and Animation:

1. Select the bin where you want to store the imported files.

2. Choose Import from the File menu to open the Import dialog.

Windows

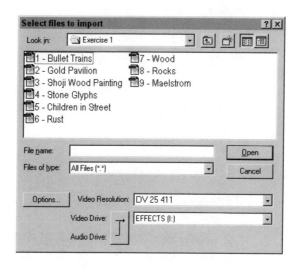

Macintosh

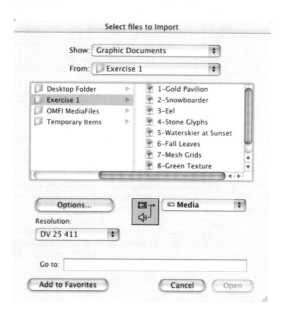

3. Navigate to the folder where the import elements are stored.

4. Select the file(s) to import.

(Windows) To select multiple files: use the Control or Shift keys to select multiple files at once. The control key allows you to select discontiguous files while the shift key allows you to select contiguous files.

(Macintosh) To select multiple files: use the Shift key to select multiple files at once.

 If the element you are importing is stored in sequential file format, only select the file for the first frame, not every frame.

5. Choose the Media Drive.

6. Click the Options button.

The Import Settings dialog box opens.

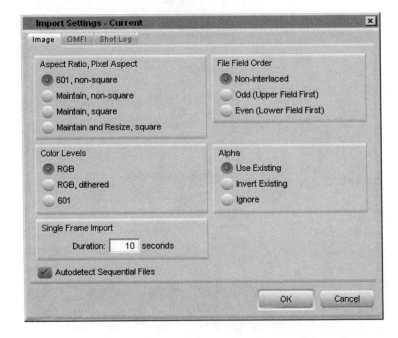

7. Use the following section to help you set the various import options.

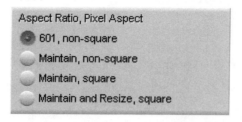

Aspect Ratio, Pixel Aspect
- 601, non-square
- Maintain, non-square
- Maintain, square
- Maintain and Resize, square

- **601, non-square** —This is the system default. This option assumes the file is properly sized for import and leaves the image alone. (Refer to the table on page 8-3 for the proper import sizes.) If the image is not properly sized, this option forces the image to fit the entire video frame, which will distort images with non-television aspect ratios.

- **Maintain, non-square** — (NTSC only) This option is designed to be used with full frame non-square NTSC images imported into an NTSC DV project. The full NTSC frame has a size of 720 x 486 (as opposed to the 720 x 480 frame size of NTSC DV). The top four lines and bottom two lines of the 720 x 486 frame are removed from the image. This conforms to the SMPTE specification for NTSC DV frames.

- **Maintain, square** — This option is designed to be used with images that are smaller than the video frame size and cannot be resized. It does not attempt to resize the image, but compensates for the square pixels, centers it within the video frame and adds video black around the image. This option is designed to make it easy to bring in small graphics, such as web-originated art, into Avid Xpress DV.

- **Maintain and Resize, square** — This option assumes an incorrect image size. It letterboxes the image with video black and resizes it to fit either the 720 pixel width (for wide images) or the 480 (NTSC) or 576 (PAL) height (for tall images). It also assumes the import file has square pixels and compensates accordingly.

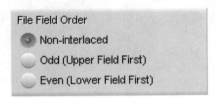

If the graphic has an alpha channel and one of the three Maintain options is chosen, the system will key out the area around the graphic instead of adding video black.

- Allows you to set the field ordering of the import file. If the file is not interlaced (frame rendered), set this option to "Non-Interlaced." Otherwise, refer to the following table to choose the correct option.

Import Created For	NTSC	PAL*
DV	Even (Lower Field First)	Even (Lower Field First)

* Field ordering in PAL-DV is different than the field ordering for PAL analog or 601 video. This is due to a difference in the standard specification.

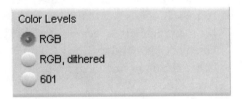

- **RGB** — This option is designed to be used with traditionally created computer images. The blackest black in the graphic will be assigned the value of video black and the whitest white will be assigned the value of video white.

  This option should be chosen for graphics and animations created in third party programs unless the graphic or animation uses 601 levels.

- **RGB, dithered** — Assigns values identically to RGB. Select this option if you are importing a graphic with a fine gradient. Due to the limitations of DV video encoding, banding is possible in fine gradients. This option adds a slight amount of noise to the gradient and masks the banding inherent in digital video.

- **601** — Use this option if the graphic was created specifically to use the extended signal range available in the ITU-R BT.601 video standard. Do not use this option if the graphic was not created with 601 levels as illegal color values may result.

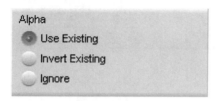

- **Use Existing** — Applies only to images that have an alpha channel; the setting has no effect on images that don't have an alpha channel.

  Use this option if the alpha channel was inverted by the graphic artist or animator.

- **Invert Existing** — Inverts the black and white areas in an alpha channel.

  Use this option when files that use the traditional designation for the alpha channel.

- **Ignore** — If this option is selected, the system disregards the alpha channel and imports only the RGB portion of the image.

8. If you are importing an animation stored in sequential file format, make sure that Autodetect Sequential Files is selected. Otherwise, only the selected frame of the sequence will be imported.

9. When you are satisfied with the Import Settings, click OK to return to the Import dialog.

10. Click OK to begin the import process.

Exporting Video as QuickTime

1. Select the desired sequence or clip in its bin.

   If there is more than one sequence or clip to export, place them in a single bin and select all of them.

2. Choose File > Export.

   The Export dialog box opens.

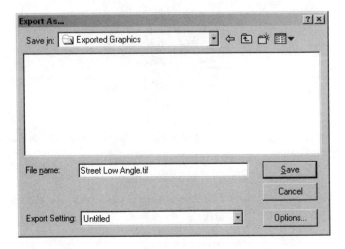

3. Click the Options button to open the Export Settings dialog box.

   The Export Settings dialog box opens.

Choosing the Correct Export Type

Two different types of QuickTime movies can be exported from Avid Xpress DV:

- QuickTime Standard — all of the media is embedded in the movie file.

  All of the media used in the sequence is copied into the QuickTime movie. As a result, the export may time a while and the exported movie may be quite large.

- QuickTime Reference — none of the media is embedded in the movie file.

  None of the media used in the sequence is copied into the resulting QuickTime movie. Instead, a small QuickTime file is created that points to the required media files on the media drives. A QuickTime Reference movie exports very quickly.

The QuickTime movie type depends upon where the movie you are exporting will be processed. Use the following table to determine the type of QuickTime movie you should use.

Movie Processed On	Shared Storage?	Use Export Type
Avid Xpress DV System	not applicable	QuickTime Reference
Other Computer System	Both systems on a shared storage network	QuickTime Reference
Other Computer System	Systems **not** on a shared storage network	QuickTime Standard

Exporting as a QuickTime Reference Movie

1. Choose QuickTime Reference from the Export As pop-up menu.

   The QuickTime Reference options appear.

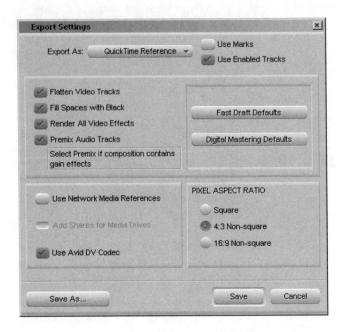

2. Use the following section to help you set the various export options.

   • **Use Marks** — If this option is selected Avid Xpress DV will only export the portion within the IN and OUT points.

   In the absence of an IN point, this option will export the entire sequence.

   • **Use Enabled Tracks** — This option controls which track(s) are exported in a multilayer sequence.

   • If Use Enabled Tracks is deselected, the video will export from the highest monitored track and the audio on all monitored audio tracks will be mixed together.

   • If Use Enabled Tracks is selected, the video will export from the highest active track and the audio on all active tracks will be mixed together.

This option is designed to allow an editor to select a large number of audio tracks and export them in a group for audio post.

- **Flatten** — If this option is selected, all of the video tracks are flattened into a single video track.

  This option should always be selected when exporting movies for external processing.

- **Fill Spaces with Black** — If this option is selected, any filler holes in the video will be replaced with video black.

  This option should always be selected when exporting movies for external processing.

- **Render All Video Effects** — If this option is selected, any unrendered effects in the sequence are rendered prior to export. If it is deselected, any unrendered effects are ignored.

  This option should always be selected when exporting movies for external processing.

- **Premix Audio Tracks** — If this option is selected, the audio is mixed down to stereo prior to export.

- **Use Network Media References** — This option should be enabled if the movie will be processed on another station that is connected to the editing station via a Unity or Unity LanShare network.

- **Add Shares for Media Drives** — This option should be enabled only if both the editing and the compression stations are on a Unity or Unity LanShare network and some of the media used by the exported movie is stored on a local drive.

  If this is not the case, leave this option deselected.

- **Pixel Aspect Ratio** — This option allows you to embed the aspect ratio of the source video into the QuickTime movie.

  Very few third party programs support this option at this time.

- **Use Avid DV Codec** — This option determines which DV codec is used to encode the exported material. If selected, the Avid DV codec is used. If deselected, the default QuickTime DV codec is used.

For more information on the Avid DV codec see "The Avid QuickTime Codecs" on page 8-29.

3. Click on the Save As... button and name this setting.

   Saving a setting allows you to easily switch between different export configurations. Use a name that makes the options easy to identify. For example, *QuickTime Reference.*

4. Click Save to close the Export Options dialog.

5. Navigate to the location you wish to save the QuickTime movie to.

6. Enter a name for the movie.

   Don't use non-alphanumeric characters, such as \ / | * ? : < > in the file name. These characters are not allowed in filenames in Windows or Unix systems.

7. Click OK to save the movie.

   Avid Xpress DV automatically adds the three-character extension, .mov, to the end of the file name.

Exporting as a QuickTime Standard Movie

1. Choose QuickTime from the Export As pop-up menu.

   The QuickTime options appear.

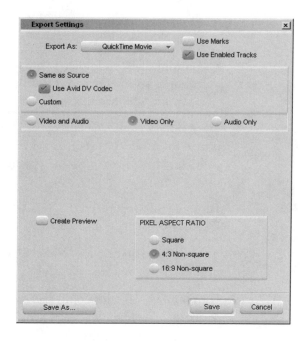

2. Use the following section to help you set the various export options.

   - **Use Marks** — If this option is selected the Avid Xpress DV will only export the portion within the IN and OUT points.

     In the absence of an IN point, this option will export the entire sequence.

   - **Use Enabled Tracks** — This option controls which track(s) are exported in a multilayer sequence.

     - If Use Enabled Tracks is deselected, the video will export from the highest monitored track and the audio on all monitored audio tracks will be mixed together.

     - If Use Enabled Tracks is selected, the video will export from the highest active track and the audio on all active tracks will be mixed together.

This option is designed to allow an editor to select a large number of audio tracks and export them in a group.

- **Compression (Same as Source / Custom)** — These two options specify how the exported movie is compressed.

  - Same as Source instructs Avid Xpress DV to export the movie using the DV codec.

  - Custom enables additional export options and allows the editor to set the size and codec used. We will discuss this option in a moment.

- **Use Avid DV Codec** — This option determines which DV codec is used to encode the exported material. If selected, the Avid DV codec is used. If deselected, the default QuickTime DV codec is used.

  For more information on the Avid DV codec see "The Avid QuickTime Codecs" on page 8-29.

- **Tracks (Video and Audio / Video Only / Audio Only)** — These options allow you to specify which tracks are to be exported.

  If your movie contains both video and audio, be sure that the Video and Audio option is selected.

- **Create Preview** — This option appends a QuickTime movie preview frame to the file.

  This data is ignored by most programs and this option can remain disabled.

- **Pixel Aspect Ratio** — This option allows you to embed the aspect ratio of the source video into the QuickTime movie.

  Very few third party programs support this option at this time.

3. Click on the Save As... button and name this setting.

   Saving a setting allows you to easily switch between different export configurations. Use a name that makes the options easy to identify. For example, *QuickTime Movie.*

4. Click Save to close the Export Options dialog.

5. Navigate to the location you wish to save the QuickTime movie to.

6. Enter a name for the movie.

Don't use non-alphanumeric characters, such as \ / | * ? : < > in the file name. These characters are not allowed in filenames in Windows or Unix systems.

7. Click OK to save the movie.

Avid Xpress DV automatically adds the three-character extension, .mov, to the end of the file name.

Setting Custom Compression Options

Selecting Custom enables additional options in the Export dialog.

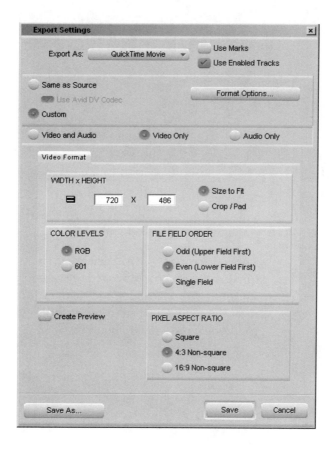

The following section discusses the options enabled.

Format Options

This button allows opens the standard QuickTime compression dialog allowing you to select the desired video and audio codecs.

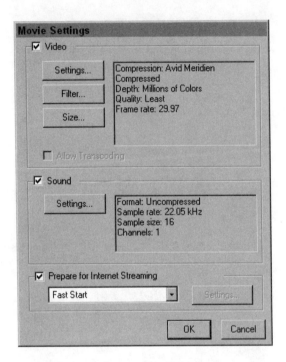

- **Video Settings** — Opens the video compression settings, allowing you to select the desired QuickTime codec and frame rate.

  The codec you choose will determine the quality and usability of the final movie. Many of the codecs are designed for specific uses, such as streaming video, graphics, and so on. The following table lists the most commonly used video codecs available with QuickTime 5. (Additional codecs may also be installed.)

Codec	Usage	Description
Avid DV	Preferred codec for DV media	Reads and write the native MPEG2 DV format (DV25 only). Provides highest level of image quality with Avid Xpress DV. Requires a frame size of 720 x 480 (NTSC) or 720 x 576 (PAL). For more information, see the following section on the Avid codecs.
DV - NTSC / DV - PAL	Preferred codec for DV media	The standard QuickTime-supplied DV codec. Requires a frame size of 720 x 480 (NTSC) or 720 x 576 (PAL). Does not support an alpha channel.
Avid Meridien Compressed / Avid Meridien Uncompressed	Compatibility with Avid Meridien-based systems	Provides the ability to read and write movies using the Meridien compression used by Avid Media Composer release 8.0 and later. Saves the video at the resolution you choose. Supports an alpha channel. For more information, see the following section on the Avid codecs.
Avid ABVB Nuvista	Compatibility with Avid ABVB-based systems	Provides the ability to read and write movies using the AVR compression used by Avid Media Composer release 7.2 and earlier. Supports an alpha channel (ABVB AVR resolutions only).
Animation	High-Quality Input/Output	Provides lossless compression at the maximum quality setting. Switches to lossy compression at lower compression settings Commonly used as an intermediate format. Can create very large files. Supports an alpha channel.
None	High-Quality Input/Output	Does not compress the file and can create very large files. Each frame is stored at full resolution. Supports an alpha channel. Not recommended for use.
Sorenson Video / Sorenson Video 3	Multimedia Output (Web or CD-ROM)	Designed primarily for web use, use this codec only for final output. Compresses very slowly. We do not recommend it for importing into or exporting from Media Composer. Unlike Cinepak, this codec requires QuickTime 3.0 for playback. Capable of producing higher quality results at lower data rates than Cinepak. See Appendix A for more information on this codec.
Component Video	High-Quality Input/Output	Transcodes the image to 4:2:2 YUV. Does not compress the frame and creates very large files. Does not support alpha channels. Not good as a delivery format.

- **Filter** — Allows you to apply a QuickTime effect filter.

  These filters are a standard part of QuickTime and will significantly increase the export time, if applied.

- **Size** — Lets you specify the export frame size.

  This option is part of the standard QuickTime interface, but is not the appropriate place to specify the export frame size.

- **Sound Settings** — Lets you specify the audio compression, sample rate, and bit depth.

  Should be set to 48 kHz, 16 bit, or 32 kHz, 16 bit to maintain full audio quality. Compression should only be used when creating final output for web or CD-ROM and is covered in Appendix A.

Video Format

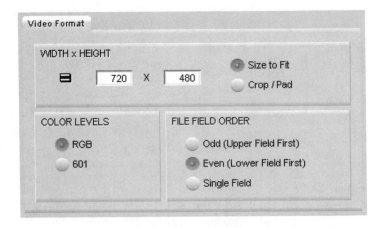

- **Width x Height** — Allows you to specify the frame size for export. Any frame size can be chosen, but the fast menu provides a list of commonly used export sizes.

- **Size to Fit** and **Crop / Pad** — If a frame size other than the native frame size is chosen, these options determine how the video frame is fit into the chosen frame size.

  - Size to Fit forces the image to fit the chosen frame size and will distort the image if a non-video aspect ratio is chosen.

- Crop / Pad does not distort the image. Instead, it either adds lines of black to fill out chosen frame size (for example, when the 720 x 486 NTSC frame size is chosen) or removes lines to fit the chosen frame size.

- **Color Levels** — Specifies the Color Levels the exported movie will contain.

- **File Field Order** — Determines the field order of the exported movie.

  - Odd (Upper Field First) and Even (Lower Field First) will adjust the field ordering, if necessary, to conform to the chosen option.

    Both the NTSC and PAL flavors of DV use Even (Lower Field First) ordering. NTSC 601 is identical, but PAL 601 uses Odd (Upper Field First) ordering. If exporting a movie that will be used in a PAL 601 project, select Odd (Upper Field First) to reorder the fields.

  - Single Field exports only the information in field 1.

The Avid QuickTime Codecs

Avid provides several QuickTime codecs that can be used to maintain the highest level of compatibility with Avid editing systems. These codecs can be used in any program that fully supports QuickTime.

Avid DV

This codec is designed to provide the highest level of compatibility with third party programs and Avid Xpress DV. DV codecs are available from various manufacturers including Avid, Apple, and Canopus and these codecs have subtle differences, particularly in the color space conversion between RGB and YUV. The Avid DV codec provides to third party programs the same color space conversion used internally by Avid Xpress DV.

When passing DV video between multiple programs (for example, between Avid Xpress DV and Adobe AfterEffects), it is important that the same color space conversion is used in every program. If different codecs are used with each program, a color space mismatch can occur and cause shifts in some colors and changes in luminance values. Therefore, it is recommended that editors and compositors use the Avid DV codec in other programs when processing video that will be imported back into Avid Xpress DV.

The Avid DV codec is installed with Avid Xpress DV and is available to all other programs on the same system. However, if you are using another system to process your movies, you will need to install the Avid DV codec on that system. An installer for the codec is located in the Goodies folder on the Avid Xpress DV Installation CD.

 The YUV color space stores an image as luminance and two color difference signals. This format is used for video as it provides storage space efficiencies versus RGB and provides a signal that can be easily read by both color and black and white televisions.

Avid Meridien Compressed and Avid Meridien Uncompressed

These codecs allow you to create QuickTime movies that use the native Avid Meridien compression. As a result, movies created using these codecs import very quickly into Avid Media Composer versions 8.0 and later and all versions of Avid Symphony.

 Movies created with the Avid QuickTime codecs must be rendered with the native frame size for the selected resolution. The following table lists the native frame sizes for all Meridien resolutions.

Resolution	NTSC Frame Size	PAL Frame Size
1:1, 2:1, 3:1, 10:1, 20:1	720 x 486	720 x 576
2:1s, 4:1s, 15:1s	352 x 243	352 x 288
4:1m, 10:1m	288 x 243	288 x 288

Configuring the Avid Meridien Codecs

The following instructions describe how to use the Avid Meridien codecs in Adobe After Effects. The process is similar for other programs, but the initial steps may be slightly different.

1. Select the composition you want to render.

2. Select Composition > Make Movie.

3. Name the file and navigate to the location where you want to save it.

   The render is added to the Render Queue.

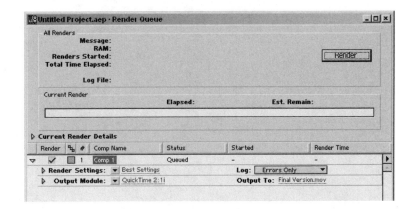

4. Click the selected Output Module to open the Output Module Settings.

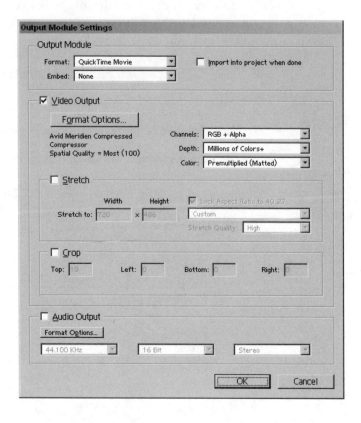

5. If creating a composite with an alpha, set the Color to Straight (Unmatted). Avid Media Composer and Avid Symphony do not support premultiplied alpha channels.

6. Select QuickTime Movie from the Format pop-up menu.

7. Click on the Format Options button to display the QuickTime compression settings dialog.

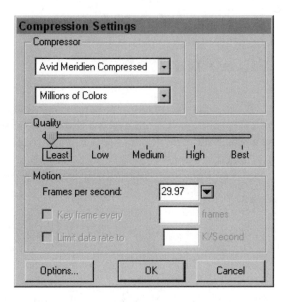

8. Select the Avid Meridien Compressed or the Avid Meridien Uncompressed codec from the Compressor pop-up menu.

9. Click the Options button to display the codec configuration dialog.

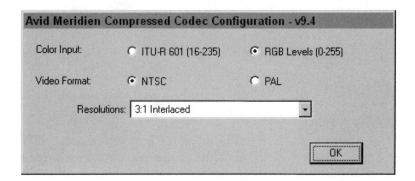

The Codec Configuration dialog allows you to set the color levels used in the movie, the video format and the resolution.

10. Choose the appropriate options and click OK to close the dialog.

11. Close the remaining dialogs and click Render in the Render Queue dialog to begin the render process.

Creating Video for Import

When creating video or animation elements for use in an Avid Xpress DV project, it is often necessary to create versions for use both in a DV project and a final online on an Avid Media Composer or Symphony. Remember that NTSC DV and 601 resolutions have different frame sizes and that PAL DV and 601 have different field orderings. Use the following guidelines when creating video or animations to be used in both DV and 601 systems.

 The following suggestions assume that the video or animation elements are created in Adobe After Effects or a system with similar output capabilities.

- Always create the video or animation at the final online frame size.

  Use the 720 x 486 NTSC 601 non-square pixel frame size, not the 720 x 480 NTSC DV frame. There is no difference between the PAL 601 and PAL DV frame sizes.

- (NTSC) Enable field rendering in the Render module and set it to Lower Field First.

- (PAL) Enable field rendering in the Render module and set it to Upper Field First.

  This sets the correct field ordering for PAL 601. We will use the Crop option to switch the ordering for PAL DV.

- (NTSC only) Create an Output module for the DV resolution and use the Crop option to remove the top four and bottom two lines from the frame.

Removing four lines from the top and two lines from the bottom ensures that the movie's field ordering is not changed.

- (PAL only) Create an Output module for the DV resolution and use the Crop option to add one line to the top and remove one line to the bottom of the frame.

This option effectively changes the field ordering by moving the rendered movie down one scan line. The line added to the top is automatically keyed out in After Effects.

- When the movie is ready to be rendered, add an output module for each desired resolution (for example Avid Meridien 2:1 and DV).

  Additional output modules can be added by selecting Composition > Add Output Module.

- Name the rendered movies to indicate the resolution of the file (for example *movie_2-1.mov, movie_DV.mov*).

Review Questions

1. What is the difference between square and nonsquare pixels? *(See "Square and Non-Square Pixels" on page 8-2.)*

2. Why does an image exported with nonsquare pixels appear distorted when you view it in Photoshop? *(See "Square and Non-Square Pixels" on page 8-2.)*

3. What is the main benefit of 601 mapping? *(See "601 Mapping" on page 8-6.)*

4. What happens if you import a graphic with RGB levels with the Media Composer set to 601 levels? *(See "601 Mapping" on page 8-6.)*

5. When is QuickTime Reference the best export option? *(See "Choosing the Correct Export Type" on page 8-19.)*

6. When is QuickTime Standard the best export option? *(See "Choosing the Correct Export Type" on page 8-19.)*

Appendix A

Preparing Video for the Internet

This appendix outlines the steps to create a QuickTime movie that can be streamed over the Internet. The steps documented in this module require Discreet Cleaner 5 in addition to the Avid editing system.

Objectives

After you complete this module, you will be able to:

- Prepare your sequence for export

- Export your sequence

- Prepare the video for Internet Streaming

- Prepare the audio for Internet Streaming

- Compress the final streaming movie.

Preparing the Video for the Internet

Though the primary distribution for most projects is still videotape and over the air broadcast, Internet distribution is becoming a common secondary, and in some cases primary, method of distribution.

If the delivery requirement includes Internet distribution, there is a very specific process the editor must go through to prepare the program for Internet distribution:

1. Prepare the sequence for export.

2. Export the sequence out of the Avid Xpress DV.

3. Process the video and audio using Cleaner 5.

4. Transmit the final file to the Internet video server or site.

This module will cover the first three parts of the process.

Preparing the Video for Export

Creating Effects

Due to the frame size of the final movie, special considerations may need to be taken if your sequence contains titles or effects. Depending upon the connection speed targeted, the frame size will be between 160 x 120 and 320 x 240. Small, subtle details and small font sizes may not be readable.

- As a general rule, modify your titles so the text point size is at least twice as large as you would use for a broadcast master.

- Avoid italicized serif fonts or fonts with fine details.

    These details may not resolve at a small frame size and the text may be difficult to read.

- Avoid any Picture-In-Picture effects that are smaller than one fourth of the frame.

Smaller PIPs can be used, but the image in the PIP may not be readable by the viewer. This is especially true for over-the-shoulder PIPs.

✍ *Expert Render the effects in your sequence before you export the sequence. If you do not, the system renders them during the export and export time may increase dramatically.*

Preparing Letterboxed Video

In some cases, you may want to present the movie at an aspect ratio other than the television standard 1.33:1. As long as you are using a standard aspect ratio, it is not necessary to apply a Mask effect to the entire sequence. The Mask can be left off and the streaming video cropped to the desired aspect ratio.

Remember, everything in the image must be compressed, even black letterbox bands. QuickTime supports any aspect ratio. There is no reason to letterbox an image within a 1.33:1 frame.

✍ *If you are using a non-standard aspect ratio, apply a Mask to the first few frames of the sequence and adjust it as necessary. These first few frames can be used to set the position of the crop in Cleaner 5.*

Preparing the Audio for Export

Unless you are creating silent QuickTime movies, preparing the audio is as important as preparing the video. Due to space considerations in the final movie, the audio will need to be significantly compressed and downsampled. (The final audio will be 4 percent of its original size or even smaller.)

Use the following guidelines when preparing your audio mix.

• Mix the audio so that the average gain is around –8 to –10 dB, digital and peaks are no more than –4 dB, digital.

Due to the high degree of audio compression required, the source audio needs to be as far away from the noise floor as possible.

- Adjust the mix so that there is minimal dynamic range.

  Dynamic range is the difference between the softest and loudest passages. Dynamic range should be reduced for two primary reasons:

  - Most streaming audio codecs do not handle wide dynamic range well.

  - Most computer users, especially corporate users, do not have high quality speakers connected to their computer. Wide dynamic range will result in either the soft passages being inaudible or the loud passages distorting.

- Mix to mono, not stereo.

  Due to the bandwidth required for stereo, it should only be used for streams that will be viewed via a high-speed broadband or local area network connection.

- Once the mix is complete, perform a mixdown and check the mixdown for clipping.

- Replace all of the source audio tracks in the sequence with the mixdown.

  Be sure to keep a copy of the sequence with the original audio tracks.

Exporting the Sequence

Once the video and audio in the sequence is ready, you can export the sequence.

1. Select the sequence in its bin.

   If there is more than one sequence to export, place them in a single bin and select all of them.

2. Choose File > Export.

The Export dialog box opens.

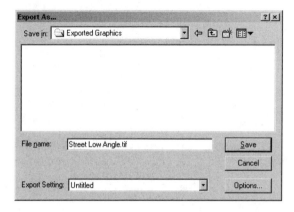

3. Click the Options button to open the Export Settings dialog box.

   The Export Settings dialog box opens.

Choosing the Correct Export Type

Two different types of QuickTime movies can be exported from Media Composer:

- QuickTime Standard — all of the media is embedded in the movie file.

  All of the media used in the sequence is copied into the QuickTime movie. As a result, the export may time a while and the exported movie may be quite large.

- QuickTime Reference — none of the media is embedded in the movie file.

  None of the media used in the sequence is copied into the resulting QuickTime movie. Instead, a small QuickTime file is created that points to the required media files on the media drives. A QuickTime Reference movie exports very quickly.

The compression chosen depends upon where the final compression will be performed and whether the editing and compression stations are networked. Use the following table to determine the type of QuickTime movie you should use.

Compression System	Shared Storage	Use Export Type
Avid Xpress DV System	not applicable	QuickTime Reference
Other Computer System	Editing and Compression systems on a shared storage network	QuickTime Reference
Other Computer System	Editing and Compression systems **not** on a shared storage network	QuickTime Standard

Exporting as a QuickTime Movie

See "Exporting Video as QuickTime" in Module 8, page 18 for the steps required to export a QuickTime movie.

Preparing and Compressing the Movie

For the final compression for the web, you should use Discreet Cleaner 5. The remainder of this module discusses the steps used in Cleaner 5 to prepare and compress the movie.

Streaming Video Considerations

When preparing video for the web, it is very important to understand that the final source video will play at a much lower data rate than it does in the Avid Xpress DV.

 Internet or network bandwidth is usually measured in kilobits or megabits per second as opposed to video editing systems which use kilobytes or megabytes per second. There are eight kilobits in a kilobyte and one thousand twenty four kilobits in a megabit.

- Uncompressed video has an approximate bit rate of 170 megabits per second.

- Uncompressed 44.1 kHz stereo audio (CD quality) has an approximate bit rate of 1.4 megabits per second.

- A cable modem has an effective streaming video throughput of 300 kilobits per second.

  This is 0.17 percent of the bandwidth required for uncompressed video or 21 percent of the bandwidth required for uncompressed stereo audio.

- A 56K modem connection has an effective streaming video throughput of 32 kilobits per second.

  This is 0.018 percent of the bandwidth required for uncompressed video or 2.2 percent of the bandwidth required for uncompressed stereo audio.

Needless to say, playing back video and audio over the web requires substantial compression.

Cleaner 5 can create streaming movies using either QuickTime, RealSystem, or Windows Media. Each streaming format has its own advantages and disadvantages. However, QuickTime supports both traditional streaming and *progressive* streaming. Progressive streaming does not require a dedicated streaming server. Instead, the movie is downloaded to the local system and then played back.

This module covers compression for QuickTime. See the Cleaner 5 manual for information on the other two streaming formats.

Preparing for Compression

1. Launch Cleaner 5.

The Batch window is automatically opened.

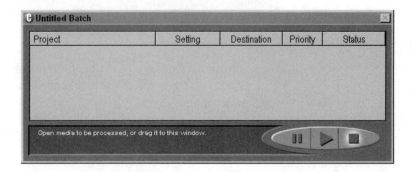

2. Locate the exported QuickTime movie and drag it into the Batch window.

   If you have more than one movie to process you can drag them in a group. Once imported the movie(s) will appear in the batch list.

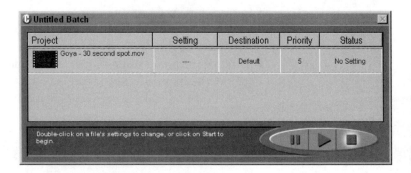

3. Double-click on the name of the movie to open the Project window.

   Cleaner 5 refers to each movie to be compressed as a project. The project window allows you to navigate through the movie and review the compression settings for the movie.

4. If you cannot see the entire window, type Control+0 (Windows) or Command+0 (Macintosh) to reduce the size of the window.

If possible, work on a system with a high-resolution monitor.

5. If your source movie is 16x9, select 16x9 from the Display Aspect Ratio pop-up menu.

6. Click on the Edit button to the right of the closed Settings pane to open the Advanced Settings window.

If the Settings Wizard window opens instead, click on the Advanced Settings button at the bottom of the Settings Wizard window.

Cleaner 5 can operate in either the Wizard or Advanced mode. We will use the Advanced mode as it offers the full range of options.

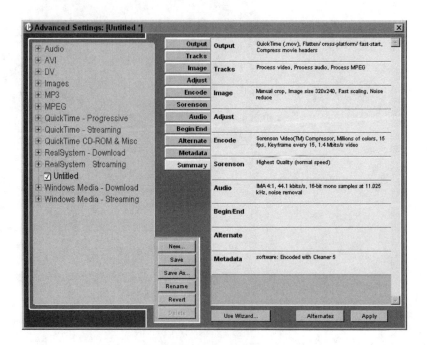

The Advanced Settings window allows you to configure how the movie will be compressed. When creating a streaming movie, many options will vary depending upon target bandwidth. This module will provide the settings for three common bandwidth targets: 56K modem, low-speed broadband and high-speed broadband.

Cropping the Movie

■ Click the Image tab in the Settings window.

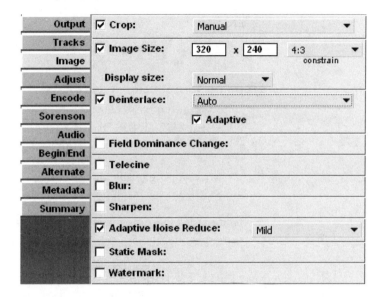

Cropping to Safe Action

If the movie was sourced from video, you should crop the movie to Safe Action. Safe Action represents the region seen by the viewer on a television. If you don't crop at Safe Action there will be too much air around any titles, which were placed within Safe Title. Additionally, cropping at Safe Title zooms in on the center of the image slightly which will result in a more readable image. Even if your movie does not contain any titles, cropping to safe action is a good idea.

1. Activate cropping by clicking the Crop checkbox and choose Numeric from the Crop pop-up menu.

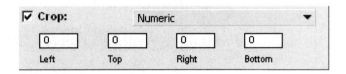

2. Refer to the following table and enter the correct crop values for your movie.

Format	Crop Left & Right	Crop Top & Bottom
NTSC	32	24
PAL	38	28

Cropping to a Specific Aspect Ratio

If your movie is letterboxed to a specific widescreen aspect ratio, you should crop to that aspect ratio instead.

1. Activate cropping by clicking the Crop checkbox and choose Numeric from the Crop pop-up menu.

2. Refer to the table following table and enter the correct crop values for your aspect ratio.

Aspect Ratio	Format	Crop Left/Right	Crop Top/Bottom
1.78:1 (16x9)	NTSC	10	62
16x9 anamorphic*	NTSC	10	13
1.66:1	NTSC	10	48
1.85:1	NTSC	10	68
2.35:1	NTSC	10	105
1.78:1 (16x9)	PAL	12	72
16x9 anamorphic*	PAL	12	16
1.66:1	PAL	12	57
1.85:1	PAL	12	80
2.35:1	PAL	12	125

16x9 anamorphic implies that the material was shot in 16x9 using the full video frame. These images must be viewed using the 16x9 mode on a monitor. 1.78:1 (16x9) implies that the material was shot in 4x3 and was letterboxed to 16x9.

Setting the Movie Size

Frame size has an important affect on video quality. When streaming movies over the web, the movie is limited to a specific bandwidth. This means that the larger the image, the lower the image quality. The Image Size section of the Image tab allows you to set the size of the movie.

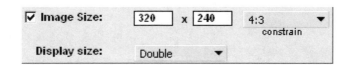

1. Enter the desired height and width.

   If your movie has the standard video aspect ratio (4x3), refer to the following table to determine the appropriate image size.

Bandwidth Target	Width	Height
56K Modem	160	120
Low-speed Broadband	192	144
High-speed Broadband	320	240

   If your movie has a widescreen aspect ratio, set the Constrain pop-up menu to the right of the image size fields to Unconstrained and refer to the following table to determine the appropriate image size.

Bandwidth Target	16x9	1.66:1	1.85:1	2.35:1
56K Modem	160 x 88	160 x 96	160 x 84	160 x 68
Low-speed Broadband	192 x 108	192 x 116	192 x 104	192 x 84
High-speed Broadband	320 x 180	320 x 192	320 x 172	320 x 136

2. If desired, choose Double from the Display Size pop-up.

   This option instructs QuickTime to automatically double the size during playback which provides a larger image to the end viewer.

Deinterlacing the Movie

As DV media contains two fields, you must use deinterlacing to remove one of the two fields. Cleaner 5 provides five deinterlacing methods: Blend, Odd, Even, Intelecine, and Auto.

1. Activate the Deinterlace option.

2. Choose a Deinterlace option from the pop-up menu using the following guidelines:

    *   If the movie was sourced from video, choose Odd, or Even.

        Both of these options will delete one of the two video fields and there is not a significant difference between the result of either choice.

    *   (NTSC only) If the movie was sourced from film, choose Intelecine.

        This option performs an intelligent inverse telecine and will remove the 2:3 pulldown introduced during the film to video transfer.

    *   (PAL only) If the movie was sourced from film, choose Blend.

        This option blends the two fields together. As both fields in PAL film transfers are from the same film frame, this option will produce the smoothest result.

3. If you are outputting a high-speed broadband movie, select Adaptive.

    The Adaptive option analyzes each video frame, and only deinterlaces those regions that have temporal differences between the two fields. This process results in a much higher quality image when the final image has a size of 320 x 240 or larger.

    Do not select Adaptive if you are outputting a lower-bandwidth movie.

Noise Reduction

One of the reasons Cleaner 5 produces such high-quality final movies is because it uses adaptive noise reduction to clean up the image prior to compression.

■ For best results, enable Noise Reduction and choose Mild from the pop-up menu.

This option removes any noise in the image while leaving object edges sharp. This results in an image that encodes more efficiently and does not look blurry.

If the video image is very noisy, choose Moderate or Extreme instead.

Adjusting Gamma (Macintosh only)

The Adjust tab allows you to adjust the image levels. Usually, the only adjustment you should concern yourself with is Gamma, which lightens or darkens the midtones of the video image without affecting the black or white point.

You should use Gamma to compensate for the gamma differences between Windows and Macintosh systems. A movie that looks fine on a Macintosh is often too dark when played on a Windows system. If you are compressing on a Macintosh and your movies are to be viewed on both platforms, you need to set Gamma so the image is acceptable on both platforms.

1. Click the Adjust tab and turn on the Gamma control.

2. Set the Gamma to 30.

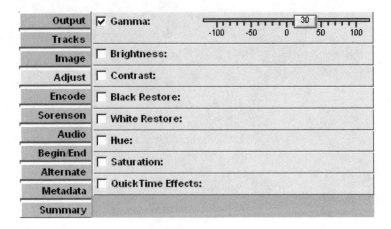

Setting the Video Encoding Options

1. Click the Encode tab to display the encoding options.

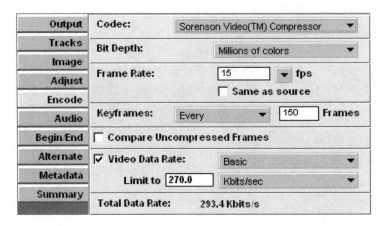

2. Choose Sorenson Video Compressor from the Codec pop-up menu.

   The Sorenson Video Compressor is specifically designed to provide good quality video at streaming data rates. Sorenson Video-encoded movies play fine on modern computers, but may not play without skipping frames on older, slower computers.

3. Set the appropriate output frame rate.

- (NTSC) Set the frame rate to 15 fps.

    If the source was film-originated and the Intelecine option was chosen, set the frame rate to 12 fps.

- (PAL) Set the frame rate to 12.5 fps.

Keyframes

The Sorenson Video codec uses both *spatial* and *temporal* compression. Spatial compression removes redundant data within an individual frame. For example, if the top of the frame is a blue sky, instead of storing every blue pixel, it notes that a region of pixels is blue.

Temporal compression only saves the differences between frames. (For example, in a picture of a talking head the first frame is spatially compressed.) It then saves only the portion of the frame that changes from frame to frame. (For example, the mouth, the eyes, and so on.)

For temporal compression to work effectively, occasional frames must be compressed spatially. These frames, known as *key frames,* are used as a reference when creating the temporally compressed frames.

■ Set the Keyframe rate to ten times the movie's final frame rate.

    For example, if your frame rate is 15 fps, set the Keyframe rate to every 150 frames.

Video Data Rate

The most important encoding option is the data rate. The entire movie's video rate must be under the available throughput for the chosen streaming bandwidth.

The following table lists the total optimal bandwidth available for the three primary bandwidth targets.

Bandwidth Target	Total Available Bandwidth
56K Modem	23 kilobits per second
Low-speed Broadband	96 kilobits per second
High-speed Broadband	300 kilobits per second

When setting the video data rate you have to reserve space for the audio.

■ Set the Data Rate Limit to the rate listed in the following table for your chosen bandwidth target.

Bandwidth Target	Video Data Rate Limit
56K Modem	16 kilobits per second
Low-speed Broadband	80 kilobits per second
High-speed Broadband	270 kilobits per second

Sorenson Video Developer Edition

Though the basic version of Sorenson Video included with QuickTime produces acceptable streaming movies, much higher quality encoded is available with the Sorenson Video Developer Edition. The Developer Edition adds many features including two-pass variable bit rate encoding and sophisticated keyframe control.

The Sorenson Video Developer Edition is available directly from Sorenson at www.sorensonvideo.com.

Setting the Audio Options

The audio settings directly impact both audio and video quality. The audio in a streaming movie must use very little of the available bandwidth or the video quality will suffer dramatically. Remember that every kilobit allocated to audio is one less kilobit available for video.

■ Click the Audio tab to display the Audio settings.

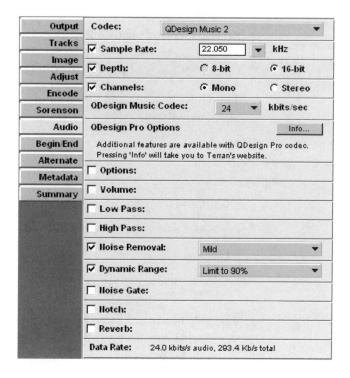

Choosing the Audio Codec

Different audio codecs are available and are optimized for different types of audio.

- If your audio is primarily music or a mix of music and voice, you should choose the QDesign Music 2 codec.

- If your audio is primarily voice, you should choose the Qualcomm PureVoice codec.

Using the QDesign Music 2 Codec

1. Choose QDesign Music 2 as the Codec.

   This codec is optimized for encoding music and can provide very high quality results with very low bandwidth usage.

2. Choose the appropriate Sample Rate using the following table for reference.

Bandwidth Target	Audio Sample Rate
56K Modem	8 kHz (see warning)
Low-speed Broadband	11.025 kHz
High-speed Broadband	22.050 kHz

 The 56K bandwidth is very limited and is not well suited for movies that contain musical content and video. When encoding audio that is primarily music, you must lower the video bandwidth to 15 kilobits.

3. Set Channels to Mono.

4. Choose the appropriate data rate using the following table for reference.

Bandwidth Target	Data Rate
56K Modem	8 kbits/second
Low-speed Broadband	12 kbits/second
High-speed Broadband	24 kbits/second

A good rule of thumb with this codec is to allocate one kilobit per kilohertz.

5. Enable the Noise Removal option and select Mild from the pop-up menu.

Even if you cannot hear any noise, you should select this option. Even the most minor audio noise will degrade the final audio. Cleaner 5 removes random white noise as well as more structured noise such as power line hum.

6. Enable the Dynamic Range option and select Narrow Range from the pop-up menu.

This option limits the peak volume to 90% of the maximum and raises the softest sounds by 20%. A reduced dynamic range is not only easier to hear on inexpensive or built-in computer speakers, but is also easier to encode.

Using the Qualcomm PureVoice Codec

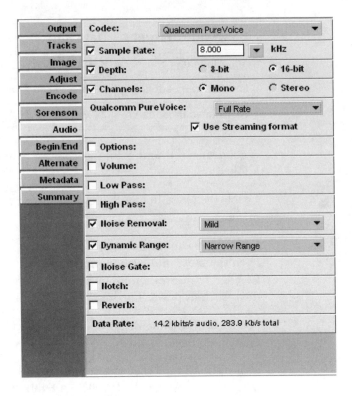

1. Choose Qualcomm PureVoice as the Codec.

   This codec is designed to encode voice in a minimal amount of bandwidth. Though it is perfect for talking heads and narration, it should not be used to encode music.

2. Choose 8 kHz as the Sample Rate.

   Only 8 kHz is supported in streaming QuickTime movies.

3. Set Channels to Mono.

4. Choose the appropriate data rate using the following table for reference.

Bandwidth Target	Data Rate
56K Modem	Half Rate
Low-speed Broadband	Full Rate
High-speed Broadband	Full Rate

5. Enable the Noise Removal option and select Mild from the pop-up menu.

   Even if you cannot hear any noise, you should select this option. Even the most minor audio noise will degrade the final audio. Cleaner 5 removes random white noise as well as more structured noise such as power line hum.

6. Enable the Dynamic Range option and select Narrow Range from the pop-up menu.

   This option limits the peak volume to 90% of the maximum and raises the softest sounds by 20%. A reduced dynamic range is not only easier to hear on inexpensive or built-in computer speakers, but is also easier to encode.

Saving the Settings

Once you have configured the settings you can save them so you can apply them to a group of movies.

1. Click on the Save As... button in the Advanced Settings window.

   The Save Setting As dialog box opens.

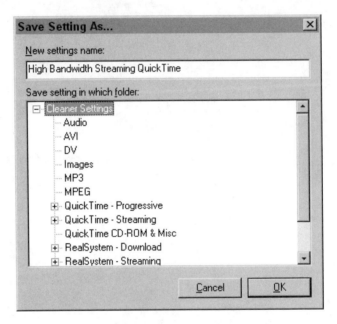

2. Enter a name for your setting.

3. Select a location for your setting.

4. Click OK to save your setting.

Final Compression

You are now ready to compress your movie.

1. Click the Summary tab to review the options you have set for the movie.

2. Click Apply in the Advanced Settings window to apply your setting to the movie.

3. If necessary, configure the settings for any additional movies.

4. Click on the Start button in the Batch window to begin processing.

On a 600 mHz Pentium III, you can expect compression time to average 12 minutes for every minute of finished video.

Once compression is complete, you will have a QuickTime movie ready to stream over the Internet.

Index

Avid Educational Services Course Offerings 08/01/02

The following list includes Avid Educational Services' current course offerings. To register for a class, receive a catalog, or find the Avid Authorized Education Center nearest you, in North America call 800-867-2843 (AVID), Worldwide call 978-275-2071. For up-to-date course schedules, visit our web site at www.avid.com/training.

*Courses with an asterisk (*) following the name are available both as an instructor-led course and a stand-alone book with exercise media on a companion CD-ROM or DVD-ROM.

**Courses with a double asterisk (**) following the name are available only as a stand-alone book (with exercise media on a companion CD-ROM or DVD-ROM) or as an interactive CD-ROM.

101 | Avid Media Composer Editing

This three-day course introduces the concepts of nonlinear editing and includes all basic features of the Avid Media Composer system for Macintosh and Windows. Session time is divided between demonstration and hands-on practice, with ample time for experimentation with sample material. Students will use Avid Media Composer to digitize and organize source footage, edit sync and non-sync material, trim sequences, edit audio, create titles, and output work. The final product will be a finished program. This course is also appropriate for Avid Symphony users. Prerequisites: Designed for the novice Avid Media Composer editor, no familiarity with the system is necessary. Completion of a Macintosh or Windows introductory course or equivalent is required, and a background in editing, production, or post-production is strongly suggested.

Editing Essentials for Avid Media Composer and Avid Xpress**

This self-paced book, with alternating content modules and hands-on exercises, provides an in-depth overview of editing techniques for Avid Media Composer and Avid Xpress. Learn how to digitize and organize source footage, edit sync and non-sync material, trim sequences, edit audio, create titles, and output work. Prerequisites: Designed for the novice Avid Media Composer or Avid Xpress user, no familiarity with the system is necessary. Completion of a Macintosh or Windows introductory course or equivalent is required, and a familiarity with the editing process is strongly suggested. The book includes instructions for Windows and Macintosh platforms.

102 | Film Editing on Avid Media Composer

This practical three-day course prepares editors and assistant editors for film editing on Avid Media and Film Composer. Each day combines instructor-led lecture, demonstration, and hands-on practice. Topics include: Understanding the telecine process, organizing a session, logging, digitizing, editing sequences, and managing system storage. In addition, participants will learn how to create EDLs, cut lists, change lists, and digital cuts. Prerequisites: This course requires little or no familiarity with Avid Media Composer. Completion of a Macintosh or Windows introductory course or equivalent is required, as well as experience in a film editing environment.

106 | Avid Educator's Workshop

This five-day course, specifically designed for educators, introduces the concepts of nonlinear editing including all basic editing features as well as an in depth overview of the techniques necessary to teach, manage, and administer the Avid Media Composer or Avid Xpress system. The course is also appropriate for Avid Xpress DV users. Session time is divided between demonstration, hands-on practice, with ample time for experimentation with sample material, and group discussions of issues relevant to educators. Participants will use the Media Composer system to digitize and organize source footage, edit sync and non-sync material, trim sequences, edit audio, create effects and titles, and output work. The last two days of the course will focus on advanced project and system management techniques, importing and exporting graphics and video, basic troubleshooting, and system maintenance. Prerequisites: The participant should be an educator (college professors and other instructors, and technical staff) with a background in video production and/or post production but not familiar with the complexity of digital nonlinear editing on the Avid Media Composer system. Completion of a Macintosh or Windows introductory course or equivalent is recommended.

110 | Introduction to Avid Media Composer Effects

This two-day course introduces basic effects and is a prerequisite for the 305 Advanced Avid Media Composer Effects and the 310 Creating Graphics and Mattes with Avid Media Composer and Adobe Photoshop course. Class time is divided between demonstration and hands-on-practice Topics include: creating multilayered effects, keyframing effects, creating effect templates, creating motion effects and timewarps, using the 3D Effects option, and nesting layers. This course is also appropriate for Avid Symphony users. Prerequisites: Students should have completed the 101 Avid Media Composer Editing course.

117 | Avid Xpress Editing

This three-day course introduces the basic features of the Avid Xpress for Macintosh and Windows systems. Class time is divided between demonstration and hands-on practice, with ample time for experimentation on sample material. Participants will use Avid Xpress to: input source footage, create and trim sequences, edit audio, create titles, and output a finished program. The course is designed for experienced or novice editors, graphic designers, or interactive media developers. Experience with Avid Xpress or other Avid systems is not necessary. Completion of a Macintosh or Windows introductory course (depending on your system) or equivalent is recommended and a background in editing, production, or postproduction is strongly suggested.

119 | Avid Xpress DV Editing*

This two-day course is an in-depth introduction to the techniques of nonlinear editing on the Avid Xpress DV system. The class progresses through all the basic phases of creating a sequence on Avid Xpress DV, including inputting source footage, assembling and trimming sequences, editing audio, creating titles, and outputting a finished program. Class time is divided between demonstration and hands-on practice. The course is designed for video editors and developers of interactive media. Prerequisites: Experience with Avid Xpress or other Avid systems is not necessary. Completion of a Windows introductory course or equivalent experience is recommended; a background in editing, production, or postproduction is also recommended.

Avid Xpress DV Training CD-ROM**

This self-paced, interactive demonstration on CD-ROM provides comprehensive instruction on the basic techniques of nonlinear editing on the Avid Xpress DV system. No previous knowledge of the Avid Xpress DV system is required.

129 | Introduction to Avid Xpress DV Effects *

This one-day course introduces basic effects and is a prerequisite for the 329 Creating Graphics for Avid Xpress DV with Adobe Photoshop course. Class time is divided between demonstration and hands-on-practice. Topics include: creating multilayered effects, keyframing effects, creating effect templates, and nesting layers. Prerequisites: Students should have completed the 119 Avid Xpress DV Editing course or have equivalent experience.

139 | Color Correction for Avid Xpress DV *

This one-day course, designed for the intermediate user, explains how to color correct a sequence on the Avid Xpress DV system. The editor will learn how to color correct each shot in a sequence, use Avid Xpress DV's internal video scopes, make sure the color and luminance are within safe broadcast limits, and create a treatment for the entire sequence. Class time is divided between demonstration and hands-on practice. Prerequisite: Completion of the 119 Avid Xpress DV Editing course or the equivalent of six months' experience editing on the system is required.

201 | Advanced Techniques for Avid Media Composer

This two-day course is designed for experienced Avid Media Composer (or Symphony) editors who want to become more productive by mastering the system's sophisticated editing features and shortcuts. Students also learn advanced techniques to help streamline system, media, and project management. Sessions include instructor-led demonstration and hands-on practice. Topics include: editing features (such as Sync Point Editing and Replace Edit), advanced trimming techniques, editing and viewing options, sync audio methods, keyboard shortcuts, user settings, and digitizing and redigitizing tips. Project, media, and system management topics include: improving Avid Media Composer performance and moving and deleting media. Prerequisites: Completion of the 101 Avid Media Composer Editing course or the equivalent of six months' experience editing on the system is required. A background as editor, assistant editor, director, or producer is necessary.

205 | Avid Media Composer Troubleshooting (Macintosh)

Avid Media Composer and Film Composer editors using the Macintosh platform will learn how to troubleshoot basic technical problems in this two-day course. Topics include: signal flow, Macintosh-related problems, software and hardware problems, and issues involving external peripheral devices. This is an ideal class for post-production facility managers, Avid Media Composer System owners, and assistant editors. Completion of the 101 Avid Media Composer Editing course or equivalent experience and an introductory Macintosh course or equivalent are required.

305 | Advanced Avid Media Composer Effects

This two-day course focuses on designing multilayered and multinested effects on Avid Media Composer for maximum quality and optimal render time. Hands-on exercises help students create and combine effects to achieve real-world results. Topics include: effect shortcuts and tips, advanced keyframing, nesting and keying, render time reduction, and effect media management. This course is also relevant for Avid Symphony users. Prerequisites: Students should have completed both 101 Avid Media Composer Editing and the 110 Introduction to

Avid Media Composer Effects courses. They should also have several months' experience on the Avid Media Composer system.

310 | Creating Graphics and Mattes with Avid Media Composer and Adobe Photoshop

Designed for the advanced Avid Media Composer editor, this three-day course demonstrates how to prepare still and moving graphics for import into Avid Media Composer. Students will also learn how to use Intraframe Editing to create paint effects and animated mattes. Class time is divided between demonstration and hands-on-practice. Topics include: preparing and importing graphics, creating and using alpha channels, layers, and matte keys, using Adobe Photoshop to treat logos and web graphics for use in a video program, and using Avid Media Composer's Paint and AniMatte effects. Third party packages used in the class include Adobe Photoshop 6.0. This course is also relevant for Avid Symphony users. Prerequisites: Completion of the 101 Media Composer Editing course and the 110 Introduction to Avid Media Composer Effects course are required.

329 | Creating Graphics for Avid Xpress DV with Adobe Photoshop*

Designed for the advanced Avid Xpress DV editor, this two-day course demonstrates how to prepare still and moving graphics for import into Avid Xpress DV. Class time is divided between demonstration and hands-on practice. Topics include: preparing and importing graphics, creating and using alpha channels, layers, and matte keys, and using Adobe Photoshop to treat logos and web graphics for use in a video program. Third party packages used in the class include Adobe Photoshop 6.0. Prerequisites: Completion of the 119 Avid Express DV Editing course and the 129 Introduction to Avid Xpress DV Effects course are required.

320 | Finishing on Avid Media Composer and Avid Symphony Systems

This two-day course introduces the principles and practices of onlining (or finishing) programs on Avid systems. The course focuses on video signal and onlining techniques for both Media Composer and Symphony systems. Students acquire a thorough working knowledge of video and audio signals, calibration techniques, and the conforming process as a whole.

324 | Avid Symphony Finishing Effects and Color Correction

Designed for the intermediate to advanced user, this two-day course teaches the editor how to perform color correction and apply Symphony-specific effects. The editor will learn how to perform shot-to-shot and secondary color correction, perform motion tracking and stabilization, perform real-time compositing using the Ultimatte keyer, reformat a program for different delivery aspect ratios, and apply pan and scan to a reformatted program.

400 Macintosh | Avid System Support for Macintosh

This five-day course is the foundation of the program for prequalified candidates pursuing certification as an Avid Certified Support Representative. Students learn techniques to minimize system downtime and maximize productivity, focusing on software problems on Media Composer systems. Lab work and role playing give students practical experience. Topics include: basic Macintosh, SCSI, storage, software and hardware troubleshooting; system software and hardware; signal flow; and system integration. After completing the class, participants will be able to identify Macintosh and Media Composer hardware and software problems, use basic tools for troubleshooting, and provide first-line support to Avid's customer base. Prerequisites: Students must first be accepted to the ACSR program by application. They also need to complete the 101, 102, 201, and 305 classes or equivalent.

400 Windows | Avid System Support for Windows

This five-day course focuses on the integration and support of Avid Symphony systems. Avid Symphony hardware components and configurations are presented and explained. Windows and Avid software are covered. Troubleshooting concepts, models and tools are also described. Lab work and exercises give students practical experience in integrating systems and applying troubleshooting techniques. Topics include: identifying, understanding, and working with PC and Avid Symphony hardware and software; installation and configuration of Avid Symphony systems; troubleshooting and resolving problems on Avid Symphony systems. Prerequisites: Students must first be accepted in to the ACSR program by application. Requires prior completion of courses including 101, 110, and 201. Also requires completion of a Windows course or the equivalent experience and successful completion of a Windows pre-test.

402 Unity | Avid Unity MediaNet System Support

This five-day course focuses on the installation, administration, and architecture of Avid Unity MediaNet. Students will learn how to connect, configure and troubleshoot Avid Unity MediaNet, as well as other products within a post-production workgroup environment such as Avid MediaManager, Avid TransferManager, and ProTools on Unity. Lab work and exercises give students practical experience in integrating systems and applying troubleshooting techniques. Topics include: identifying and understand installation, configuration and troubleshooting procedures for Avid Unity MediaNet, Avid MediaManager and Avid TransferManager; working with networking hardware and software; and identifying hardware and software necessary to run ProTools on Unity. Prerequisites: Students must have Macintosh and/or Windows ACSR active status.

403 | Avid Unity for News

This two-day course teaches you how to install, administer, and troubleshoot broadcast products often found in an Avid Unity MediaNet news environment. Students must have Macintosh and/or Windows ACSR active status. This course is offered only as an add-on to the 402 course.

410 Macintosh | ACSR Macintosh Recertification

This two-day course focuses on the new technologies, software, and hardware that a current Avid Certified Support Representative (ACSR | Macintosh) may not be familiar with. Students will learn about new and updated topics relating to Avid Macintosh based systems. Prerequisite: Students must be Avid Certified Support Representatives (ACSRs) to participate.

410 Windows | ACSR Windows Recertification

This two-day course focuses on the new technologies, software, and hardware that a current Avid Certified Support Representative (ACSR | Windows) may not be familiar with. Students will learn about new and updated topics relating to Avid Windows-based systems. Prerequisite: Students must be Avid Certified Support Representatives (ACSRs) to participate.

500 | The Avid Master Editor Workshop

This intensive 5-day course provides a select group of editors a concentrated learning environment, focusing on ways to improve technical proficiency and enhance the creative application of the Avid Media Composer system capabilities. Highly respected special guest speakers and industry professionals will share their unique approaches to the art and technique of editing, focusing on the innovative use of nonlinear editing in the film and television industry. Potential students must submit an application and demo reel to be reviewed by Educational Services Workshop Review Committee. Please contact Avid Educational Services for additional information.

T3-101 | Train-the-Trainer: Avid Media Composer, Xpress, and Xpress DV Editing

As part of the Avid Certified Instructor (ACI) program, this five-day course prepares instructional professionals to teach the 101 Avid Media Composer Editing, 117 Avid Xpress Editing, and 119 Avid Xpress DV Editing courses. Students acquire the teaching skills through lecture, interactive role playing, hands-on sessions, and written and oral examinations. Topics of discussion include presentation skills, course curriculum, and teaching methodology. The instructor will show beginning instructors how to give presentations, lead hands-on exercises, and answer questions about Avid products from a diverse audience. During the class, students review and present course modules on inputting material into the system, editing a sequence, and outputting a finished program. Prerequisites: Students must first be accepted to the class by application.

135 | Introduction to Digidesign ProTools

This course introduces ProTools basic recording and editing functions. It is designed for audio engineers and editors who want to learn the ProTools feature set and incorporate its use into their audio and video applications. This three-day course features instructor-led demonstrations and student exercises. Topics include: recording audio; nonlinear editing; editing narration and sound effects; hardware system overview, using SMPTE timecode and fades; and managing regions and tracks. During the class, students will conduct a basic audio-editing session including inputting source material, editing tracks, and adding effects. Prerequisites: This course is for editors, audio/video engineers broadcast professionals and musicians. It requires basic Macintosh skills and a general understanding of audio and/or acoustics. Note: Mixing and the use of plug-ins are not covered in this course.

235 | Digidesign Pro Tools Mixing

This two-day course is designed for audio engineers, editors and musicians who want to learn how to effectively use the Digidesign Pro Tools mixing feature set and to incorporate it into audio and video applications. Topics include: Applying AudioSuite and TDM plug-ins; using Inserts and Sends; submixing and bouncing tracks; recording, editing, and creating automation, conducting a basic Digidesign Pro Tools mixdown and layback. Prerequisites: This is an intermediate level course. It is recommended for editors, audio engineers and musicians. Students must have completed 135 Introduction to Digidesign Pro Tools Editing prior to taking this course or have equivalent knowledge. A basic understanding of mixing boards and prior mixing experience is helpful.

DS-101 | Avid|DS Editing and Basic Effects

This three day course introduces students to the Avid|DS SD and HD workflow processes. Students will familiarize themselves with the Avid|DS editing, audio, and media management techniques. They will also get an introduction to Effects and Animation. Topics include: Capturing media, Story-boarding, Editing a scene with dialogue, Multicamera Editing, Transitions, Media Management, DVE, Color Correction, Titling, Customizing the interface, Audio Effects, Mixing Audio, and Conforming. Prerequisites: None.

DS-120 | Conforming on Avid|DS for Avid Media Composer Editors

Designed for the experienced Avid Media Composer editor, this one-day class teaches how to conform Avid Media Composer sequences on Avid|DS. Topics include: Preparing for the Avid|DS conform, conforming in High Definition, understanding how effects conform, and manipulating effects and graphics in Avid|DS. Prerequisites: Students should have completed the DS-101 course and be experienced Avid Media Composer editors.

DS-201 | Avid|DS Graphics and Effects

This two day course introduces the students to more advanced Graphics, Effects, and animation techniques. Topics include: Multiple Effects and Animation, Effects tree, Handwriting, Scratch removal, Warp Effect, Timewarping, Mix and Match, Luma Keyer, Blue/Green Keyer, and Advanced Titling. Prerequisites

DS-301 | Avid|DS Compositing and Effects

This three-day course explores the compositing and graphic tools used in Avid|DS system. Students will become familiar with the compositing and the 3D DVE layouts and workflow. Specific features of the Graphics layout are also covered. Topics include: Blue Green Keyer, Multiple Mattes, Photoshop Import, Travelling Matte, Morphing, Stabilizing, Tracking, Offset Tracking, and 3D DVE Compositing. Prerequisites: DS-201

172 | Introduction to Avid NewsCutter

This two-day course is an introduction to Avid's Windows-based news editor Avid NewsCutter Effects. This course is designed to familiarize students with the concepts of nonlinear editing. It progresses through all the basic features of the Avid NewsCutter Effects system. Students will learn to identify and execute basic steps, to input information into the system, and to output a finished program. Topics include: Recording directly to the Timeline, tape-to-disk editing, audio with keyframe action, creating digital recordings, organizing source footage, trimming edits, editing audio and outputting work. Prerequisites: Students should have prior knowledge of editing in a news environment, and be familiar with the Windows operating system. Course is limited to two students per system, maximum eight students per class. Offered on-site at customer facility only.